Teaching Writing in Kindergarten

Randee Bergen

SCHOLASTIC

NEW YORK • TORONTO • LONDON • AUCKLAND • SYDNEY
MEXICO CITY • NEW DELHI • HONG KONG • BUENOS AIRES

Dedication

This book is dedicated to all my kindergarten students,

including my daughters, Adelynn and Amelia.

It is you who taught me all I know about writing instruction in the kindergarten classroom.

May the potential of kindergarten students never be underestimated or remain undiscovered.

Acknowledgments

I would like to thank the following individuals

for their invaluable assistance, support, and inspiration.

Mary Arends	Shirlie Lohof
Betty Bearss	Sarah Longhi
Adelynn Bergen	Mel Mendez
Amelia Bergen	Jamie McClellan
Marianne Bergen	Meri Nofzinger
Mike Bergen	Cindy Pangell
Tracie Chapman	Cindy Pearson
Nancy Cozart	Connie Peterson
Suzy Danielson	Beth Roberts
Mary Anne Dibella	Sandy Robertson
Trish Donovan	Barb Salomon
Micki Frederick	Debbie Steele
Beverly Horyza	Gwen Vann

Edited by Sarah Longhi

Cover design by Jason Robinson
Interior design by Solas
Illustrations by Manuel Rivera, Paige Billin-Frye, Maxie Chambliss, Steve Cox, and Sue Dennen

ISBN-13 978-0-545-05400-3
ISBN-10 0-545-05400-1

Contents

Chapter One

Teaching Writing in Kindergarten: An Overview

To be honest, I used to be apprehensive of kindergartners. For the first 12 years of my teaching career, as I taught special education and gained experience as a classroom teacher at every other elementary grade, it never once crossed my mind that I might one day teach—or want to teach—kindergarten. However, as my own two daughters neared kindergarten age, I began to realize how readily this age group learns—and how exciting it is to watch their rapid growth in all areas, especially in language and literacy.

At about the time that my trepidation of teaching kindergarten-age children was subsiding, the opportunity to change grade levels and teach kindergarten presented itself. Intrigued by the challenge, as well as by the possibility of teaching my own daughters during their kindergarten years, I agreed to give it a try. The summer before my move to a kindergarten classroom, I searched for all kinds of professional literature about teaching kindergartners. I found a lot of strategies and ideas for teaching social skills and thematic units, but, unfortunately, I found nothing comprehensive enough to show me exactly how to teach literacy in kindergarten—one of my biggest concerns. What would be the best approach to teaching kindergartners the names and sounds of letters when these concepts are abstract and might hold very little meaning for them?

My hunch was that focused, highly structured, and meaningul instruction that was very visually and physically engaging would be the key to getting my students—many of whom would be entering my classroom with very limited literacy skills—to learn. It seemed like the immediate and daily opportunity to apply information such as letter names, sounds, and sight words might result in faster learning, better retention, and a greater understanding of how letters are used to make words and convey ideas. So I spent that summer really teaching my preschool-age daughters how to write. At the same time, they were providing invaluable insight on what children their age were truly capable of demonstrating in written language. Every day, the girls and I drew pictures together and wrote phonetic labels and ideas about the pictures. By the end of the summer, my oldest daughter, who with her late August birthday was starting kindergarten at age four, was independently writing phrases with phonetic spellings and my younger daughter, not yet four, was capable of isolating and recording beginning sounds. I attributed their rapidly developing early writing skills to the explicit instruction and daily opportunity to write during the summer.

As I embarked on my first year of teaching kindergarten, I hypothesized that by providing conditions similar to those I had provided for my daughters—structure, high expectations, explicit and scaffolded individualized instruction, and daily meaningful writing opportunities—I could create a whole classroom full of enthusiastic and fluent kindergarten writers.

Now, several years later, I am thrilled to report that those students, and the many others I have since taught, proved me correct. Not only do most students meet—and in many cases exceed—typical kindergarten expectations (see page 125 for an end-of-the-year assessment results chart for my most recent full-day/every-day kindergarten class), the writing they produce is so extraordinary that I have collected their writing samples, shared my ideas with colleagues, and fully developed my approach to how I teach writing in the kindergarten classroom.

ABOUT THIS BOOK

Teaching Writing in Kindergarten shares my approach in a comprehensive and practical yearlong guide designed just for kindergarten teachers and their students. Every facet of teaching beginning writing is addressed, from what to do the first day when students hardly understand the notion of writing, to helping them develop a correct pencil grasp and neat handwriting, to individualizing instruction so students can progress at their own pace with no ceiling of opportunity. In addition to being effective, the ideas in this book are practical. You'll find that great writing instruction requires not much more than 30 minutes a day, pencil, and paper. Advance lesson planning is minimal, given that a key element to this approach is analyzing students' writing as they are working and deriving instructional points on the spot.

The book is based on sound theory and years of classroom success. Perhaps the most compelling evidence you'll see, however, is in the dozens of writing samples I include from the children I've worked with—all from a variety of backgrounds and beginning-of-year skill levels. Their impressive writing provides evidence that a much higher level of writing proficiency can be expected from students at this age than has been expected of them in the past. By raising our expectations and strategically nurturing the growth of students' early literacy skills, we may ultimately redefine what constitutes best practice at the kindergarten level.

In addition to yielding highly developed written language skills, daily writing instruction as described in this book results in more rapid and advanced reading development than we've previously assumed is possible at the kindergarten level. This method immediately introduces and encourages the use of phonemic awareness, phonics, and the learning and application of common letter chunks. The built-in daily practice and individualized support provided during writing time will result in students learning quickly to encode written English. And, once they grasp the sophisticated process of encoding, most will easily pick up the less cognitively demanding skill of decoding required for reading.

Before committing to a daily writing program in your kindergarten classroom, you'll want to understand the basic premises of the program and to see the big picture. The guiding principles of this approach (page 8) and the yearlong plan for implementation (page 9) give you a sense of the goals and expectations, as well as the general scope and sequence for teaching writing in kindergarten. The specific strategies, procedures, and timelines for implementation are thoroughly discussed in Chapters 2 through 6.

An Approach to Fit Every Teaching Situation

The daily writing approach outlined here has proven to be effective year after year, regardless of students' skill levels (students are not expected to have prior knowledge of letters or experience with written language)—and it's adaptable for all types of kindergarten programs. Though the yearlong plan is written for a traditional nine-month school year, it can easily be applied to a year-round school calendar. Likewise, because this approach was initially developed in half-day kindergarten classes and then implemented in full-day classes, you may use it confidently in either situation.

As you read on, I invite you to consider this approach in light of your professional knowledge base and experience as a teacher of young children. You'll need to determine which aspects of the daily writing instruction to adopt as described and which to modify to complement your teaching style and address your current teaching situation and your students' needs. Above all, I hope that you enjoy the process of reflecting upon your current practice and pondering a fresh approach to teaching writing in the kindergarten classroom.

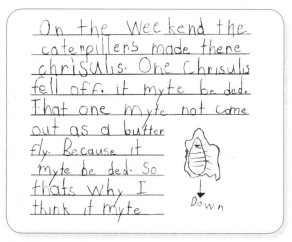

Camille, age 5 Sample from a child in a full-day/every-day kindergarten program.

10 Guiding Principles for Teaching Writing in Kindergarten

As I have developed and refined this approach to teaching kindergarten students to write, the following beliefs and practices have become the foundation of my teaching. They are the keys to cultivating students' advanced writing development.

1. Establish and remain committed to a daily writing time of 25 to 30 minutes.

2. Set high expectations for each student every writing period; have confidence that students will rise to meet these expectations.

3. For the first six weeks of the school year, provide direct, whole-group instruction in drawing, labeling pictures, and writing simple sentences, with the students copying your work onto their own paper.

4. After the first six weeks, begin independent journal writing. Deliver most instruction through individualized mini-lessons based on individual needs and goals, rather than via whole-group mini-lessons. Utilize the GLOW, GROW, SO formula: Acknowledge at least one positive aspect of the student's writing (GLOW), point out how the student can improve upon his or her writing (GROW), and request that the student immediately try to implement the information or skill (SO). Accomplish this by circulating quickly and continuously among students during writing time.

5. Provide highly structured routines to support students in this early phase of learning to encode language. A key routine is providing a daily topic until students are truly ready to write well with their own topic choice.

6. Teach students at their individual skill level and encourage them to progress at their own rate with no ceiling of opportunity. Carry out ongoing assessment through the daily analysis of student writing to support your teaching.

7. To move students steadily along the continuum of learning, use Vygotsky's (1978) zone of proximal development in combination with Bruner and Sherwood's (1975) concept of scaffolding. Simply put, recognize what a student is capable of doing today and build upon that knowledge, using intentional, temporary, and flexible supports and approaches to teach new skills at the next higher level. It is crucial to expect a little bit more each and every day.

8. Create closure each and every day. No student is permitted to be finished with writing until you determine that the student has worked up to his or her potential or to the expectations customized for that student that day.

9. Keep parents informed about your classroom writing instruction and encourage the immediate and continual appreciation of the development of their child's writing by sending students' writing home on a regular basis.

10. Publish student writing to stimulate enthusiasm, stamina, productivity, and a rapid increase in writing skills, and to celebrate all that has been learned.

The Yearlong Plan

August–September* For the first six weeks of school, whole-group direct instruction serves as a way to quickly introduce the concept of writing and the beginning skills needed for writing.

- Establish a daily writing time of 25 to 30 minutes.
- Engage students in whole-group, guided journal writing.
- Model, step-by-step, how to draw a simple picture and write a one-word label or a short phrase or sentence to accompany the picture.
- Have students copy your work, step-by-step, onto their own paper.
- Prepare students to write independently in the very near future.
- Send papers home regularly as a means of communicating with parents about the writing instruction that is happening in the classroom.

October–January After about six weeks, independent writing begins, as does customized instruction for each student. Students' writing skills will gradually and greatly improve over the next few months.

- Begin independent writing, during which students write independently in their own journals.
- Provide a daily writing topic.
- Teach mainly through brief, individualized mini-lessons.
- Support students as they write at their instructional level and progress at their own rate, challenging them as they are ready, with no ceiling of opportunity.
- Bring concrete closure to each student's daily writing; writing does not carry over to subsequent days.

February–April During these months, students' stamina, enthusiasm, and writing skills reach new heights as their writing is published as books.

- Support students as they continue to write independently in their journals.
- Provide a daily topic for writing; students are encouraged to use the provided topic but also may use a topic of their own choosing.
- Teach mainly through brief, individualized mini-lessons.
- Give students the option of carrying writing over from one day to the next.
- Publish student writing in books.
- Provide opportunities for students to illustrate, share, and read repeatedly the books they have written.
- Plan a celebration to recognize students' published works.

May As the publishing of student writing winds down and the end of the year approaches, students need extra motivation to continue advancing their writing skills.

- Provide a variety of writing topics and projects designed to maintain students' interest and proficiencies.

*This yearlong calendar is based on a mid-August-through-May school year. Teachers who begin teaching in September may simply adjust their plan forward by two weeks.

Chapter Two

Getting Started: August–September

Perhaps the most distinctive aspect of this approach to teaching writing in kindergarten is the whole-group, explicit instruction in drawing and writing that occurs during the first six weeks of the school year. Unique and highly structured, this initial instruction establishes the foundation upon which young writers grow toward independence. This chapter will explain how to plan and prepare for, and then kick-off your daily writing with whole-group writing lessons. According to the Yearlong Plan (page 9), teaching writing during the first six weeks of your year will entail:

- Establishing a daily writing time of 25 to 30 minutes.

- Engaging students in whole-group guided writing.

- Modeling, step-by-step, how to draw a simple picture and write a one-word label or a short phrase or sentence to accompany the picture.

- Having students copy your work, step-by-step, onto their own papers.

- Preparing students to write independently in the very near future.

- Sending papers home regularly as a means of communicating with parents about the writing instruction that is happening in the classroom.

ESTABLISHING DAILY WRITING TIME

The first and most vital aspect of this portion of the yearlong plan is to establish the time and expectation for daily writing. Designate a 25- to 30-minute block of time as journal-writing time and start, preferably, on the first day of school. If there are back-to-school events that prevent you from introducing the daily schedule in your classroom on the first day, or if you prefer to do some getting-to-know-you activities instead, writing instruction should begin on the second day at the very latest.

If you have not previously expected kindergartners to write this early in the school year or if students come to you having had minimal opportunities to draw or write, this suggestion may sound overwhelming. Remember, however, that kindergartners are coming to school with a *tabula rasa*, a blank slate, with no idea of what to anticipate. This provides you the perfect opportunity to define kindergarten as a place of engaged learning, which includes a regular block of time devoted to writing. Capitalizing on the very nature of kindergartners—their wanting to do what is expected of them in this new setting called school—will allow you to lead them in writing instruction on the first day. If you set the standard for students to sit, follow your directions, and try their hardest for 30 minutes, most students will do just that.

While it may seem next to impossible to find an extra half-hour for writing in your classroom schedule, rest assured you will be covering quite a bit of curriculum during this time. The writing instruction you'll offer provides practice in:

- following directions
- planning
- copying
- strategy use
- phonemic awareness
- application of phonics
- rhyming
- spelling
- letter formation
- sentence structure
- grammar

- vocabulary
- counting and other math skills
- staying on topic
- staying on task
- pencil grasp
- fine motor muscle development
- fine motor control
- drawing
- organizing

- revising
- editing
- using classroom resources
- physical stamina
- time management
- focusing
- self-monitoring
- goal-setting
- oral sharing
- listening
- reading

All of these skills can be incorporated into the daily writing time and you can list those that you are focusing on in your lesson plans.

On the other hand, if you've tried or thought about using a workshop-style approach to teaching writing, you may feel that a 30-minute period seems too brief for all that you want to accomplish. Keep in mind that beginning writers generally need much more guidance and practice than a loosely structured writing-workshop approach offers. Elements like whole-group mini-lessons and unstructured writing and sharing time not only demand more time than we can usually allot in our schedules, they also require more unfocused work time than most of our kindergartners are capable of handling. In contrast, the approach I describe gets students engaged in writing from the first minute on the first day—at first by having them follow you closely and gradually by enabling them to write independently with the support of individualized mini-lessons. The publishing process is introduced much later in the year (see February–April in the Yearlong Plan), when students have the skills to write complete ideas coherently and confidently. This means that the entire 30-minute period is reserved for actual writing. And, since students are expected to be focused and productive for the entire time, a half-hour is about as much as they can handle at this age.

Contemplate your schedule and consider your options for securing a 30-minute block of time for writing. Be creative, resourceful, and willing to experiment a little.

Sample Kindergarten Daily Schedule
(Half-day program)

A.M. session		P.M. session
8:20 – 8:45	Writing	12:10 – 12:35
8:45 – 9:05	Opening/calendar	1:05 – 1:25
9:05 – 9:50	Centers (includes guided reading)	2:20 – 3:05
9:55 – 10:20	Specials (P.E., music, library)	12:40 – 1:05
10:20 – 10:35	Recess	1:25 – 1:40
10:40 – 11:15	Whole-group activities (any content area)	1:45 – 2:20
11:20	Dismissal	3:10

Sample Kindergarten Daily Schedule
(Full-day program)

8:20 – 8:50	Writing
8:50 – 9:05	Opening
9:05 – 9:50	Morning centers (includes guided reading)
9:55 – 10:20	Specials (P.E., music, library)
10:20 – 10:35	Morning recess
10:40 – 11:05	Whole-group activities (any content area)
11:05 – 11:10	Hand-washing
11:10 – 12:00	Lunch/recess
12:00 – 12:25	Shared reading
12:25 – 12:55	Down time/independent reading/individual or small-group tutoring
12:55 – 1:15	Read-aloud
1:15 – 1:35	Afternoon recess
1:40 – 2:20	Calendar/math
2:20 – 3:05	Afternoon centers
3:10	Dismissal

Instituting the first half-hour the students are in the classroom as writing time, as shown in the schedules above, works particularly well. Students hurry in and get seated immediately, ready to hear the writing topic for the day. If writing happens first thing, students interpret it as being the most important event of the day and, supported by the teaching approach you will learn here, they soon develop a passion for writing.

Morning or Afternoon?

Scheduling writing at the beginning of the kindergarten session results in no wasted learning time. While students are getting settled and beginning to write, you will have time to conduct necessary housekeeping tasks. For example, students can get started on their writing while you take attendance, complete the lunch count, or converse with parents who are lingering in the classroom. You will still have many opportunities for personalized conversation with students as you circulate and work individually with them several times during each writing period.

Of course, daily writing can be equally exciting and effective if it must be scheduled later in the day. Ultimately, you need a block of time that will rarely be interrupted and can be reserved as sacred daily writing time. The important thing is to create the time and expectation that you will be teaching writing and students will be learning to write every single day of the school year from the beginning.

ARRANGING YOUR CLASSROOM TO SUPPORT WRITING INSTRUCTION

Many kindergarten programs include writing time, but often it is scheduled at one of several centers where only five to ten students will be writing at the same time. In contrast, you will need to determine how to have all of your students write simultaneously. The most practical suggestion is to arrange your classroom so all students can comfortably sit at tables and easily see your written instruction, whether it takes place on the overhead, chalkboard, chart paper, or a dry erase board. If this idea sounds a little impractical and foreign to you, keep in mind that you are not restructuring your entire kindergarten program. There will still be time for centers, group time, and movement activities during the day.

There are several ways to retain specific aspects of your room arrangement while also creating space for all your students to be at tables at once. Some kindergarten classrooms have a large circle area in the middle of the room, often delineated by a design or pattern on the carpet, that makes the middle of the classroom a natural gathering place for group activities. If your classroom is like this, or you have always brought your students to the center of the room for group time, consider moving your meeting area to a corner to create space in the center of your classroom for tables and chairs. Corners are cozy, contain active children well, and have the added benefit of having at least two walls for hanging instructional materials as visual references.

Do you have permanent centers set up in your room? If so, think about which of these could be condensed and stored in a folder, plastic bag, or box. Then, when you want students to participate in a stored center activity, take it out and place it at one or more of the tables you will now have set up. You might like this idea so much that you end up packing away many of your center activities and pulling them out only when you actually want the students to use them. Most of your

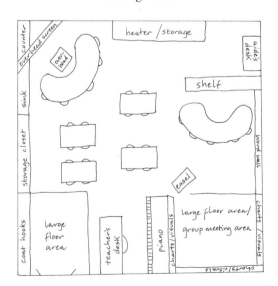

A sample classroom map shows a seating arrangement that supports whole-class lessons at the overhead (upper left corner).

centers would now consist of activities that could be done almost anywhere, as shown in the map on page 13, rather than being permanent places in the classroom.

When arranging tables, do not be too concerned about whether every chair faces the instruction directly. Kindergartners are quite flexible and can twist back and forth easily in their chairs between watching you and then copying onto their own papers. Of course, you will need to keep those students who struggle with copying close to you and always facing the instruction. Likewise, you may want to have students pull up extra chairs to a spot where they can see better and let them be a little crowded for the 30-minute period.

If it still does not seem possible at this point for you to arrange your classroom so all students can sit comfortably at tables to write, the next best option is to have as many students as possible at tables and the rest gathered close to you on the floor or in extra chairs. These students can use clipboards or large sturdy books for pressing upon. Alternate daily the students who work at the tables so everyone has a chance to sit in all areas.

Probably the least desirable option, but still an option, would be moving tables after writing time into an arrangement you need for the next activity. Rarely are conditions in our classrooms ideal; we just get creative and do the best with what we have. (For more on seating arrangements, see page 17.)

Classroom tables are arranged so all students can see the overhead during writing instruction.

LESSON SYNOPSIS FOR THE FIRST SIX WEEKS OF SCHOOL

Writing time during the first six weeks of school will consist of whole-group direct instruction. Each writing period will be divided into four main parts:

- **Writing Names** Students write their names on their papers, practicing the correct way in which their name should be written and learning the letters that comprise their names.

- **Drawing the Picture** The teacher draws a picture, step-by-step, and students copy the picture onto their papers, step-by-step.

- **Labeling the Picture** The teacher demonstrates how to write a one-word label, short phrase, or short sentence step-by-step, and students copy this model step-by-step. The teacher models, and the students practice pointing to and reading the word(s) to review what they've written and confirm that it makes sense (a key reading objective, too).

- **Creating Closure** The teacher creates closure by taking one final look at each student's paper to be certain that the student has participated to the best of his or her ability.

While the framework for each daily lesson during the first six weeks of school is basically the same, there is a gradual shift in time and focus from name-writing instruction and practice to guiding students to pay attention and learn how to copy a drawing to basic writing skills instruction. Also, in the beginning you will use a slower instructional pace as you introduce the notion of writing to students, and, admittedly, deal with frequent interruptions that have to do with beginning-of-the-year classroom and behavior management matters. Instruction becomes faster-paced and more interactive within just a few weeks. The chart below outlines the progression of instruction and instructional content in your daily writing time over the six week period. To see this progression in action, compare the sample mid-August lesson (page 27) with the sample lesson from late September (page 29).

Instructional Shifts During Daily Writing: First Six Weeks of School

Minute	Component	Week One	Week Two	Week Three	Week Four	Week Five	Week Six	Minute
1–9	Writing Name on Paper	Students use name cards to copy their names onto their papers. Teacher circulates, assisting students in copying their names just as they appear on the name card. Letter height and formation is mentioned as appropriate.	Students write their names on their papers, referring to their name cards if need be. Teacher circulates and assists with letter height and formation. Teacher begins teaching the names of the letters in each student's first name.	Students write their names on their papers. Teacher circulates and assists. Teacher continues teaching letter names in first names and begins assessing students' knowledge of the letters in their names.	Students write their names on their papers. Teacher circulates, teaching and assessing letter names in first names with those students who do not yet know them all.	Students write their names on their papers. Teacher checks and assesses letter names with those students who do not yet know them all.	Students write their names. Teacher assesses letter names with those students who do not yet know them.	1–9
10–16	Drawing a Picture	Teacher draws a simple picture, step-by-step, pausing between steps. Students copy onto their papers. Teacher circulates and assists as needed. The teacher simultaneously works on developing attention and listening skills.	Teacher draws a more detailed picture, step-by-step, using more advanced language. Students copy. Teacher circulates, providing assistance and feedback. Teacher continues to teach good learning habits.	Teacher draws a picture, asking for and including details and ideas suggested by students. Students copy. Teacher circulates, providing assistance and feedback. Teacher continues to teach good learning skills.	Teacher draws a picture, including details and ideas suggested by students. Students copy. Teacher begins to emphasize putting the drawing at the bottom of the paper. Teacher comments on good learning skills.	Teacher draws a picture, including students' ideas for details. Emphasis on drawing at the bottom and writing at the top of the paper. Teacher continues to recognize good learning behaviors.	Teacher draws a picture, including students' ideas. Emphasis on drawing at the bottom and writing at the top. Teacher continues to teach and recognize good learning behaviors.	10–16
17–24	Writing a Label, Phrase, or Sentence	Teacher models segmentation and writing letters for a one-word label. Students copy.	Teacher models segmentation and finding/writing the letters for two-word phrases—one known word, one unknown word. Students copy.	Teacher models segmentation and finding/writing the letters for two-word phrases suggested by students. Emphasis on letter formation. Students copy.	Teacher lets students try segmenting sounds and naming letters while modeling the writing of two- or three-word phrases. Emphasis on letter formation. Students copy.	Teacher lets students try segmenting sounds and naming letters before modeling the writing of a short sentence. Emphasis on letter formation and height. Students copy. Teacher points and reads the words as they are written.	Teacher lets students try segmenting sounds and naming letters before modeling the writing of a short sentence. Emphasis on letter formation and height as well as pointing to and reading the words as they are being written to ensure meaning.	17–24
25	Closure	Teacher models how to point to the word and read it. Students do it. Teacher circulates, putting a star on each student's paper to indicate closure.	Teacher models how to point to the words and read them. Students do it. Teacher circulates, putting a star on each student's paper to indicate closure.	Teacher models how to point to the words and read them. Students do it. Teacher circulates, putting a star on each student's paper to indicate closure.	Teacher models how to point to the words and read them. Students do it. Teacher circulates, putting a star on each student's paper to indicate closure.	Teacher models how to point to the words and read the sentence. Students do it. Teacher circulates, putting a star on each student's paper to indicate closure.	Teacher models how to point to the words and read the sentence. Students do it. Teacher circulates, putting a star on each student's paper to indicate closure.	25
Example	Picture	bee	face	human figure	bear	dog	traffic light	Example
Example	Writing	*B, be, bee, bzzz*	*a fas, the fac*	*a man, the grl*	*the brown bar*	*I see a dog.*	*The lit is red.*	Example

MATERIALS PREPARATION

Teaching kindergartners to write via this approach requires minimal preparation and can be done with materials you likely have on hand. Basically, all that is required is a sturdy, transportable name card for each student, paper, and pencils.

Name Cards

Before the first day of school, prepare a large, laminated name card for each student. Commercial name cards that have a top line, bottom line, and dotted middle line are available. Lined sentence strips cut to the length of each name work equally well, and are sometimes even better for names that are extra long. Since a common curricular target for kindergarten students is to recognize their first names in print, you'll want to write their names the way they will usually see them, with a capital letter at the beginning and lowercase for all subsequent letters. In this way, we start with the correct model and skip altogether the stage of writing names using entirely capital letters. The name cards you make will not be permanently attached to anything such as desks, tables, or walls. If possible, laminate the name cards you create because the students will be handling them frequently.

Placement of Name Cards

Either keep the name cards in a pocket chart that is easily accessible to students and close to the area in which they enter the classroom or unpack, or place the name cards on student desks or tables.

- **Pocket Charts**   Place the name cards in a random order so that the names appear in different locations in the pocket chart each day. As students come in, have them locate their name cards and take them to any available chair. Pocket charts can be hung on portable stands, attached to closet doors or walls using nails, or stapled firmly to bulletin boards that are at the students' level. If you do not have an extra pocket chart or a place where students can safely reach one, an alternative is to put the name cards on an empty table top where students can easily see and collect their cards.

- **Student Desks/Tables**   If you prefer to have more control over student seating, place one student name card at each seat, varying the placement of the names from day to day. When students enter the classroom, they will search for their names and sit in the correct seats.

For both options, students initially use the name cards as a guide to help them write their names, the first goal of the writing period.

Classroom Alphabets

A kindergarten classroom should have, from day one, an alphabet strip or alphabet chart that has attractive and easily recognizable pictures for each letter sound. It is helpful to have several alphabets posted around the room and it is okay if they have different pictures to represent the letter sounds. For example, a picture alphabet posted on the wall may show a hat for *Hh,* while an alphabet chart that is kept near a small-group instruction area might have a house for *Hh.* Different students will key into different pictures or resources in the classroom to aid them in the process of finding the letters they need, and sometimes the more resources that are available, the better the results.

When considering a picture alphabet to use, check each of the pictures carefully to ensure that they do indeed represent the true and most common sound of each letter and are pictures for which most students will know the names. When it comes to the vowels, it is most helpful if there is a picture representing the short sound of the vowel (an apple for *Aa* instead of an apron for *Aa*), because most students are able to quickly match long vowel sounds to the appropriate letters without much support, but have more trouble matching short vowel sounds to their letters. This is where the picture support is needed. You'll find ideas for using picture alphabets to support writing instruction on pages 39–41.

Paper

Almost any type of paper can be used at this point in the school year. I use plain white paper, but colored paper or paper with faint lines such as loose-leaf notebook paper works fine too. (Using different types of paper and switching back and forth between types of paper during these initial six weeks does not seem to be distracting for students or take away from their learning in any significant way.) Place one sheet of paper at each chair or onto each clipboard if clipboards are being used. When you place the paper on the tables, be sure to orient it horizontally. This allows more room for writing long names and for printing large letters, as kindergartners often do at the beginning of the year.

Pencils

Collect all pencils that students bring in as school supplies and dole them out as needed. For each table or work area in your classroom, have an attractive can or box with several sharpened pencils that are ready to use. Always have a few more pencils in the can than the number of students at the table in case a lead breaks in the middle of the lesson. Teach students to put pencils with broken or dull leads back in the can and to take another pencil so that they avoid interrupting the lesson or their writing time to use the sharpener.

That's it for materials preparation. Be sure each morning before students arrive that name cards are prepared and in place, there is a picture alphabet to which you and the students can refer during instruction, paper is available and laid out, and pencils with erasers are sharpened and accessible to students.

START WITH THE RIGHT TOOLS

Encourage students to use pencils and erasers, the standard writing tools, from the beginning of their instruction in writing. Some teachers encourage kindergartners to use markers as the primary writing tool and to cross out mistakes, usually with a great big X. This does not make sense. Markers, because they glide across the paper, require far less hand strength and therefore are not as helpful in developing fine motor muscle and control. Additionally, using markers and crossing out mistakes fosters impulsivity. When students are required to erase and fix their mistakes, they learn early on that it is so much easier to think first and make a plan before putting something down on paper than it is to go back and erase. The use of pencils and erasers decreases impulsivity and improves a child's ability to plan and then execute the plan.

CONDUCTING A WHOLE-GROUP WRITING LESSON

This section explains the basic framework for the whole-group writing instruction you will conduct each day during the first six weeks. It helps you clearly understand the four main components of a lesson—writing names, drawing a picture, labeling the picture, and creating closure—and how to structure and manage them. It may be helpful to refer back to the lesson synopsis and the chart with the instructional shifts (pages 15 and 16), as well as to look ahead to the sample whole-group drawing and writing lessons from mid-August and late September (pages 27–29) before delving into this section. Also, immediately following this section you'll find detailed teaching ideas for supporting the concepts that you will be introducing and teaching to your students.

Writing Names

When students enter the classroom for the day, encourage them to quickly and quietly hang up their backpacks and then steer them (literally, perhaps, until they have the routine down) toward the place where you have put the name cards. Ask them to find their names. For those who do not know what to do, point to their name cards, specifically the first letter in their names, and say something along the lines of, "This is your name. It says *Robin*. You have to look for the *R*." You will notice that the students who have already seen their names in print may still just key into the first letter and grab another name that begins with the same letter. When this happens, show them how to look beyond the first letter for other salient features in their names. For example, you may show a child that his or her name has two *l*'s right together in the middle. Or you may point out that his or her name is very long.

Students should take their name cards from the pocket chart to any seat in the room where they see a piece of paper. With this procedure, students are free to choose where they want to sit; since the name cards are not attached to any tables or desks, there is no assigned seating. As mentioned earlier, an alternative method that allows you a little more control over where students sit is to place the name cards, along with the writing paper, at the tables. Students enter the room, look for their names, and sit in their chairs.

Supporting Students as They Write Their Names

The next step is for students to copy their names onto their papers. Some students will know how to write their names already and some will have no idea how to pick up a pencil and get started. One of the main expectations to emphasize here is that every student should try to copy his or her name exactly the way it appears on the name card, with a capital letter at the beginning followed by lowercase letters. The name cards will give the more experienced students something to think about as they try to write their names precisely the way they appear on the name cards, and also serve as a great support for the students who do not yet know how to write their names. For students who are completely unable at this point to copy the letters on their name card, slip the name card beneath the paper and show them how to trace the letters. Wean them from this support when you feel they should begin to attempt copying instead of just tracing.

There will not be much time at this point to speak to students about correct letter formation. On the other hand,

> **PAPER POSITION ALERT!**
>
> Keep an eye out for papers that may get turned out of position as students are getting seated, and try to turn them back to a horizontal format before students begin to write.

it is never too early to start mentioning how certain letters should be formed. In fact, sometimes it is the frequent repeating of letter formation cues that will help a student the most in writing his or her name in a timely manner and in remembering the letter names and what the letters look like. There is a discussion on developing correct letter formation, along with letter formation cues, on pages 42–46. Also, in Chapters 6 and 7, you can find strategies to use with students who are still struggling with their handwriting later in the year.

Circulating to Each Student

While students are getting their names onto their papers, circulate about the room a few times and assist as needed. The goal here is not for everyone's name to be perfect, not on the first day, anyway. Rather, point out one or two things that each student should think about and work on for now. Instructional points may range from adjusting a pencil grip to locating which letter to start with (and that might be the only letter that gets onto the paper that day) to learning that the lowercase *y* in a name hangs down further than the other letters.

Circulating to each student at least twice allows you an opportunity to provide feedback on what you asked them to do the first time you talked to them. If you make a habit of checking back with students they will soon learn that they are accountable for following through with what is requested of them. Circulating twice works particularly well with students who work slowly or are less focused. You can use a comment such as "I want to see that *D* on your paper the next time I come by."

Creating Closure on Writing Names

Develop a system or routine, such as putting a star on students' papers next to their names, and use it consistently from day to day, to let them know that they are finished. Finished for some students may mean the name is written completely and correctly. For others, it will imply that they did what you asked of them and what was expected for that day. For that slower student, if he or she had a *D* written down when you checked back and it was time to move on with the lesson, he or she should get a star, too. The star on the paper provides not only a sense of closure for each student for that portion of the lesson, but it is also, for you, a visible means of ensuring that you have checked back with all students and are satisfied with what they have produced. The star also indicates to a student that he or she is finished with the name card for now and can return it to the designated spot for name cards. As you take a final look at names, assist students who are not going to be able to complete their names or who did not write legibly. The process of writing their names out for them on their papers serves as a model for students and helps you identify to whom the paper belongs.

The first few days of writing names on papers are hectic, to be sure. In fact, writing time may be half over if you do not keep a close eye on the clock and move the lesson along. Rest assured that it will take only a few days for the majority of your class to learn to legibly write their names on their own within a few minutes, leaving more time for you to focus on the other students. While this is a good opportunity to practice writing names, getting students to write their names perfectly is not the ultimate objective of your writing lesson. If you find that after a few days the majority of your writing time is still being devoted to name writing, try to make a conscious effort to expect a little less from the students and put stars next to their names in a more timely fashion in order to move on. This is not to suggest that you let their mistakes or a lack of progress go unnoticed; you will need to schedule time during other parts of the day for students to practice writing their names correctly.

Drawing the Picture

When all students have their names on their papers to your satisfaction, you can announce the writing topic for the day. *Announce* is a key word here because, after a few days of drawing instruction, your students will be excited to find out what they get to learn to draw next and will greatly anticipate the announcement of such.

Be sure you have the attention of every student as you think aloud and draw each step of the picture. Periodically, walk around the room to be sure every student is keeping up, and then model the next step in the drawing and circulate, if needed, again. Repeat this until the drawing is complete. You can see how this is done in the mid-August sample lesson and again in the late-September sample lesson (pages 27 and 29). As you read through and compare these two lessons, you will see that the skills, concepts, and language used for the September lesson are considerably more advanced. The pace of the lesson is faster, too, with less explaining and less circulating. This is because the students' abilities to pay attention, take risks, and copy what you are doing will improve dramatically within just a few weeks.

When the drawing portion of the lesson is over, all students should have recognizable pictures on their papers. You may help them draw, hand over hand, when necessary; or, with certain students who need a lot of support, you may need to draw most of the picture for them at first. If you must do this, make a conscious effort to do it less each day while encouraging the students to do more for themselves. One of the best ways to get students to try more of the drawing on their own is to repeat a favorite drawing a few times during the first six weeks. The students' ability to draw that one thing really well is what some students will rely on when you tell them in October, "Today you are going to draw and write something all by yourself."

Choosing a Picture to Draw

One of the most surprising aspects of this daily writing approach is that it is so effective in developing basic writing skills in young writers, yet it demands very little planning or preparation time. For the first six weeks of the school year, planning will consist of carefully choosing a picture to draw, which the students will copy, and creating a label or sentence to put with the picture. Each day you will need to have not only a picture in mind and an appropriate label, but also some idea of how you are going to break the picture into drawing steps. Since students will be copying you step-by-step, you will need to know these steps in advance.

NAME CARDS: AN ATTENDANCE TOOL

As students become more capable of coming in and getting started on their own, you will find that scheduling writing as the first event of the day provides the perfect time for you to take attendance, complete a lunch count if necessary, and attend to the arrival issues that always seem to walk in along with the students. A quick way to determine who is absent is to check which name cards are remaining in the pocket chart while students are working on their names. Taking attendance in this manner wastes no learning time. If you take this approach, be sure to make it a policy that students will take their name cards out of the pocket chart whether they still need to copy from them or not. When they have gotten a star by their names and the okay to return their name cards to the pocket chart, the process has gone full circle and the names are ready for the next school day.

Joe, age 6 The Busy Bee is the class mascot in my kindergarten room, so I teach the students to draw a bee and I repeat this topic often during writing time. Note that Joe could easily draw and write about the topic given for the first day of independent journal writing on October 4th because we had practiced it several times during guided writing the first six weeks of school.

WHY SPEND TIME TEACHING STUDENTS TO DRAW?

The reasons for providing instruction in drawing are myriad and far-reaching. Having students think about and notice details in pictures helps them become more observant about the world around them. If you discuss how the window you are about to draw is shaped like a square, you will catch several students checking the windows in your classroom to see if they really are shaped like squares. Prior to this, students may not have paid attention to the windows, much less considered their geometric properties. They may even begin to look at and compare the shape of other things in the classroom with those windows in mind. When you model how to draw a picture, you show students how to break a whole into its individual parts. You are using, in a very authentic manner, important math terms and concepts. You will find yourself saying things such as, "Draw a circle on the right side of the square," or "Next, you make a straight line above the first line you drew; this line should be a little bit longer."

When students copy your drawing, they create a concrete representation to which they all can relate. Bear in mind that some kindergarten students have never been shown how to draw before. For them, watching a picture unfold on the overhead is delightful. They are motivated to pay attention, watch carefully, and try their hardest to copy exactly what you do, making this the perfect time to incorporate the teaching of these important learning skills. If students only copied letters and words, and these things were not yet meaningful to them, they might not expend the same effort or show the same enthusiasm. You will see the thrill on your students' faces and the pride they have in their drawings, which will gradually come through in their writing, too.

If you are at all concerned about drawing simple pictures, then having a reference drawing to copy, breaking the picture into steps for yourself, and practicing the drawing ahead of time if need be, will adequately mask any lack of skill or talent in this area. Useful contour line drawings can be found in children's books, teacher materials, or clip art collections. Keep in mind, too, that this age group will be accepting of your artistic ability, whatever it may be.

In addition to selecting a simple subject that you are capable of drawing, the picture you select may also be related in some way to something important that is currently happening or that your students are studying in the classroom. In other words, seize the opportunity to integrate a classroom pet or theme, words or concepts from a social-studies or science unit, or something else that is meaningful and timely for you and your students. While drawing and waiting for students to copy your model, there will be time to converse about the topic, providing a nice opportunity for discussion and review.

Examples of topics for drawing and writing during the first six weeks of school are shown at right. You can tell from these samples that my drawings are simplistic and appeal to children. This helps students to follow along and produce quality pictures of their own.

Labeling the Picture

A label is a single word that tells about the picture that is drawn on the paper. It works best, in the beginning, to help students hear and isolate the first sound of a word and write the one letter for that sound. If time allows, or when the students seem ready, write the two most prominent sounds in the one-word label. Eventually, you'll be able to help them record all the sounds heard in the word you have chosen for that day. As an example, one of the students' favorite drawings in my class is the Busy Bee. The Busy Bee is the special helper of the day, and the class uses several chants, songs, and pictures of the Busy Bee on a daily basis. The picture is a little complicated to draw the first day, but it's perfect for teaching sound-letter correspondence when it comes time to label. The students can clearly hear the letter name and so initially we record just the letter *B* as a label (see the example below). A few days later, students can draw the bee again and write *bz* or *be* because these labels add just one more sound to a familiar letter-sound.

Sample Pictures and Accompanying Labels

Teacher's Drawing	Label	Reasoning	Student Sample
	B	The Busy Bee is our class mascot, and students will draw it and write about it throughout the year. Its label, a single phoneme, is a good one to start with on the first day.	
	bat	Students already know the /b/ sound. *Bat* encourages simple segmentation with three distinct phonemes.	
	sad	Faces and expressions provide many opportunities for different labels, from simple (*fas* or *sad*) to more complex (*The grl is mad*).	
	me	Learning to draw a human figure teaches children to notice the body's structure as well as the details, such as hair style and clothing. This label is a sight word that had just been introduced.	
	the cro	Students should practice two-word phrases after they've practiced with one-word labels. This topic reflects students' interest in a book I shared with the class about crows. *The* is a familiar sight word on our word wall.	
	I see a bus.	By the end of the first six weeks, many students are ready to write simple sentences using both familiar sight words (*I, see, a*) and one or two unfamiliar words they must sound out (*bus*).	

Choosing a Label

When planning, be sure to choose pictures that begin with a distinct consonant or long vowel sound and also have clear and easy-to-hear subsequent sounds. The words you choose should have four or fewer phonemes.

It is important to point out that you will not be modeling conventional spelling of words at this point, except for instances when you are using perfectly phonetic words or high-frequency words that have already been introduced and taught. You will always only record the letters that represent the actual phonemes heard. The word *face*, which is used in the sample mid-August lesson, has three distinct phonemes. For the most part, students will understand what you are doing when you show them how to write an *f* for the /*f*/ sound, an *a* for the /*ā*/ sound, and an *s* or *c* for the /*s*/ sound. *Shoe*, on the other hand, would not be a good choice for this time of year because the /*sh*/ and /*oo*/ sounds will only confuse the students. The chart below provides several good one-word labels and shows how to segment, count, and record the sounds.

One-Word Labels That Are Perfect for Phoneme Segmentation

These one-word labels are easy to break into simple phonemes and work well for writing lessons you might teach in the first six weeks. To help students segment the sounds, put up one finger for each sound that can be heard. The letters beneath each hand picture are the only letters that you should write when you demonstrate how to label the picture. To see a model lesson in action with phoneme segmentation, see the sample lessons starting on page 27.

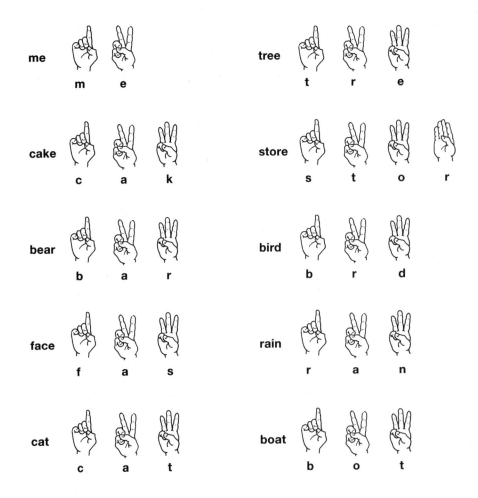

me   m e

tree   t r e

cake   c a k

store   s t o r

bear   b a r

bird   b r d

face   f a s

rain   r a n

cat   c a t

boat   b o t

Writing Phrases and Sentences

It will not be long before students know how to write their names and copy your drawings quickly. Suddenly you are left with ten minutes to spend on actual writing during guided writing time. When this happens, take advantage of it by introducing how to write a short phrase and eventually a complete sentence. The opportunity should present itself around the third or fourth week of school.

Skills that support phrase and sentence writing may include:

- formulating the sentence and picturing it in one's mind before trying to write it
- putting finger spaces between the words as they are written
- executing return sweeps
- pointing to the words to reread and check what has been written

Again, the goal at this point is not complete understanding or mastery, so you can limit the discussion and rush the modeling a bit to fit it into your 30-minute lesson, if need be. While your students may not completely grasp these skills during the first six weeks of learning how to write, having plenty of opportunities to watch you demonstrate sentence writing will prepare them to try it on their own when they are ready.

As a transition between one-word labels and sentences, model two-word phrases for your students. These two-word phrases should include one word that they know and one that will require listening to and writing down the sounds that can be heard. Examples include: *the man, a bot* (for *a boat*) and *one brd* (for *one bird*), wherein the first word is one that students know how to write because it has been taught and the second word is unfamiliar in print and requires sound segmentation. (See Two Ways to Write a Word on page 32 for teaching tips.)

When you move to sentences, what you choose to model should be short, concrete, include one or two high-frequency words that you have already introduced, and also incorporate one or two words with sounds that are easy to segment and record. If the picture is an apple, the sentence might be, *The apple is red,* and it would be written, *The apl is red.* Let's say you have drawn a dog. You could suggest the sentence, *A dog can bark,* and write, *A dog can brk.* The sentences you choose should reflect what you have already introduced to your students, which means you need to start introducing and teaching sight words early in the school year so students have a base of known words to use while writing.

As you start involving students in the process of formulating a sentence to use, they may suggest more sophisticated sentences that are too long and complicated. When this happens, take the student's idea and count the words on your fingers. Assure the student that it is a good sentence but that right now you just do not have time to write a sentence with that many words. It will not be long before students learn to give you shorter, more manageable ideas that they can attempt to write.

By transitioning from the modeling of one-word labels to short phrases and, finally, complete sentences, students will feel more comfortable writing to their potential when independent writing begins in October. If you do not model sentence writing on several occasions while you are doing whole-group instruction, your students will tend to write one-word labels in their independent writing journals for a longer period of time and will have more difficulty moving into the writing of sentences.

Creating Closure on the Whole-Group Drawing and Writing Lesson

A major component of this approach to implementing daily writing in kindergarten is to bring concrete closure to each daily writing session for each student. This means that students receive feedback from you, which will help them sense that their writing is finished or completed to the best of their ability. Obtaining closure lets students know that they have worked up to their potential and met your standards for that day, and this feeling allows them to more easily move on to the next activity. Helping students reach closure day after day is the primary way of teaching students how to realize their potential and how to meet it daily as the year goes on.

You can help students get the impression they are finished, as well as provide an easy means for ensuring that everyone actually has finished, by using a quick visual cue. Just as it was suggested that each student get a star next to his or her name once he or she has finished satisfactorily, you can do one of a few things to indicate to yourself which students have finished the drawing and writing portion of the lesson to your expectations. As you circulate around the classroom between steps in the drawing and writing, make sure that all students are keeping up. Then, when the lesson has come to an end, you will only need to briefly circulate one last time and check the last step students were supposed to do. Another strategy is to put a sticker, a second star, or a smiley face on students' papers when they have drawn the picture and written the way you want them to. A quick glance at the papers to see if any students do not yet have a star will indicate to you with whom you still need to follow up. Any of these methods will help you determine who still needs your attention before that sense of closure can be obtained.

To not implement this closure component and allow kindergarten students to be finished or to turn in their work without first getting your approval is to do them a disservice. It is important to reiterate every day that work is never "done" unless it is done to the best of one's ability and to the standard set by the teacher. Students will learn quickly what your expectations are if their work has to be approved by you before it is considered finished. As the year goes on, your students will adopt your standards, and they will more readily work up to their potential.

Sample Guided Writing Lesson Mid-August

The students are finishing up with writing their names on their papers, and the drawing lesson is about to start.

Creating Closure on Writing Names

"Is there anyone who doesn't have a star by your name? Remember, when I put a star next to your name it means that you wrote your name as best you could and tried to make it look the way it looks on your name card."

"Are you ready to draw? I can tell if you're ready because you'll be looking at the overhead and listening to each word I say."

Announcing the Topic

"Today we're going to draw a face. Oh, good, I see lots of smiles. Let's make a face that is smiling."

Drawing the Picture

"Think about your own face. What shape is your face?" I call on a few students. "Yes, that's right. Faces are shaped like circles or ovals. Watch me draw an oval on the overhead. Watch how I start at the top, circle back this way, and then am very careful when I come around because I want to make sure my lines hook together neatly at the top. Can you make a neat oval like mine?" I circulate and assist students who are having trouble making an oval.

"Now, what are some things you think we should put on this oval to make it look like a face?" I get ideas from the class until most facial features have been mentioned.

"Let's start with the eyes. How many eyes do people have? Yes, two. Our eyes are in the middle of our face. Watch me draw two eyes. I am putting them in the middle of the oval, not way up here on the forehead. Now you draw two eyes. Try to make them the same size."

"Let's put the ears on next. The reason is because the ears go straight across from the eyes. I want you to look at a friend sitting by you and see if their ears are really straight across from their eyes." I draw an imaginary line from my own eyes to my ears to demonstrate. "Okay, eyes up here. I can't draw my ears until everyone is watching. Do you see how I am going straight over from the eye and making a round bump for the ear? Now I'll do the other side. Okay, you try it." I circulate to make sure everyone is keeping up.

"Remember, we're making a happy face. What do we need to show that this person is happy? Yes! A smile! Smiles are curved lines. Watch." I draw a smile on the overhead only when all students are watching. "Your turn to draw a smile."

"Let's put the nose on. It's just a dot, like this. That's easy."

"Now for the fun part. We get to add hair. People have all kinds of different hair. Some hair covers up people's ears and some hair doesn't. Look at the friends sitting by you and see if their ears are showing." I wait for students to make their observations. "Today I am going to teach you how to draw short hair. The hair we draw will look kind of like Anthony's and Dane's and Tanner's. Do their ears show? Yes, they do, so I have to be careful not to put hair on top of the ears. Eyes up here. Here I go." I draw short back and forth motions from one ear, around the top of the oval, to the other ear. "Don't worry if you were hoping we'd do a different type of hair. We're going to draw faces in our class a lot and each time we do we'll try some different hairdos. Now it's your turn to draw short hair." Once again, I move about the room to check students' progress and assist as needed.

Labeling the Picture

"Now that we've drawn our picture, what should we do next? Who remembers? That's right! We're going to write a word. Our word has to match our picture. What did we draw? A face? So what word should we write? Yes, *face*. Let's write the word *face*."

"Watch me count the sounds. Then you can try it with me. Watch and listen—that's the only way to learn how to do it." I put my fist in the air to show that I am starting with zero. "/f/" My index finger goes up. "/ā/" I put up my middle finger. "/s/" I put up my ring finger. "How many sounds did I hear? Yes, three. I know it was three because I have three fingers up in the air. Okay, let's try it together. Start with zero. Hands up high so I can watch you. I want to make sure everyone is doing it right. Here we go." I repeat with the students the sound segmentation I just modeled for them.

Students actively follow along with me, using their fingers to count the three phonemes.

"Now we have to write the letters by our picture. Let's do the first sound all by itself. Ready? /f/ What did you hear? What letter do you think that is? You think it's an *f*? We better check to see if you're right. Let's check with the picture alphabet. Does *ffface* sound like *fffish*? Yes, it does, so it really must be *f*. Now, watch closely. I am going to show you how to make an *f*. I can't start until all eyes are on the overhead screen. Okay, here I go. I'm starting at the top, going up, curving around, and making a straight line down. Now I will lift my pen and draw a short line across, like this. Okay, it's your turn. Good luck!" I circulate and check to see that everyone gets a recognizable *f* on their papers.

I repeat these steps for segmenting, counting, and recording the next two phonemes in *face*. Students record the letters *a* and then *s* (or *c*, if a student happens to suggest it).

"After we write something, we have to read it to be sure it really says what we wanted it to say. Get your reading finger ready to point to the word you wrote. Are you ready? Here we go! *Face*." I deliberately and emphatically point to the word I wrote at the exact time I say it. I watch the students closely to make sure they all do the same.

Creating Closure on Drawing and Writing

"I'm coming around to see how you did on your drawing and your writing today. If it looks like you tried your hardest, then I'll put a star on your paper." Since I have circulated several times throughout the lesson to provide assistance and ensure that all students were keeping up and doing quality work, it does not take me long to determine that everyone's work is worthy of a star.

My completed drawing with label.

Sample Guided Journal Writing Lesson Late September

The students are finishing up with writing their names on their papers, and the drawing lesson is about to start.

Creating Closure on Writing Names

"Did each of you write your name perfectly? I hope so. I'm going to check it in a while when I walk around the room to look at your drawing."

Announcing the Topic

"Today we're drawing a traffic light. We've talked about traffic lights, and we even practiced crossing the street using the traffic light."

Drawing the Picture

"What shape should we draw for a traffic light?" I call on a few students. "Everyone thinks it would be good to start with a rectangle. Remember, rectangles have four sides—two are short and two are long." I draw a rectangle while talking. "Did you notice I put my rectangle at the bottom so I'll have room for words at the top? Try to draw really straight lines when you make your rectangle and be sure it hooks together as you finish." I circulate to assist and to check students' name writing.

"I can tell you're ready for the next step because your eyes are on the overhead. You look ready to listen and learn! What should we do next?" Again, I solicit a few ideas from students. "Let's draw three very round circles that are the same size and have spaces between them. None of our circles should touch. Don't draw your circles yet; watch me draw mine first. I'm going to start with the top circle, which is the red light. Circles are like o's, so I'm going to make sure I start at the top of my circle and circle back. You check to see if I do it right. Now I have to close my circle up neatly. I'll try to make my second circle the exact same size as my first. That's how traffic lights look. Start at the top and circle back. Okay, one more circle. Now it's your turn. Take your time and do them neatly. I'm coming around to watch you." I move about the room, trying to observe each student make at least one circle and assessing if the students start the circles at the top and circle backward instead of forward.

"Now, let's make the red light shining. Which circle is the red light? Yes, it's the top one. How can we make it look like it's shining? We have to think like artists. What would an artist do?" I call on a few students. "Good idea. Let's put lines around it, kind of like the rays that come out of the sun. Be careful with your lines. Keep things under control and make nice, straight lines."

Writing a Sentence

"Okay, I think we're ready to write a sentence that goes with our picture. Any ideas?" I call on students and gather ideas. I choose a simple sentence that includes a detail about the light's color. "I like the way this idea describes our picture: *The light is red.* Let me tell you why. It has some words we already know and can just write down and it also has some words that we'll need to listen to carefully so we can hear the sounds. Those are two very important things we practice during writing time. Let's say the sentence together and count the words on our fingers." I show my fist, indicating zero; the students do the same. The students and I say the sentence and put up one finger for each word. "I see four fingers, so this sentence has four words."

"The first word is *the*. Is *the* a word we know? Yes, it is. All we need to do is write it down, or, if we can't remember how to do it, look on the word wall. Who can show us where *the* is on the word wall?" I call on a student to point to *the* on the word wall and I make sure that all students see where it is.

"My turn first. Eyes up here. I'm going to start with a capital *T* because it's the beginning of our sentence. I'll start at the top, go straight down, then hop to the top and draw a line across. Can you tell I tried to make the lines on my *T* very straight? Okay, your turn to make a capital *T*." I wait until the students have finished making a *T* and all eyes are on me or the overhead screen before proceeding. "Next is *h*. I'll start at the top again. Watch and listen, so you can make your *h* just like mine. Down, trace it up, with a bump. Your turn. Here I come to watch you." I walk around the room, helping students form the *h* correctly. "Now it's time for *e*. Do you remember what we say when we make a lowercase *e*? Straight across and around. I want you to say 'straight across and around' when you make your *e*. Good luck!"

Again, I move about the room, knowing that some of the students will concentrate and try the proper letter formation only if they know I am watching them. When they are ready, I say, "Okay, let's touch this word and read it." The students and I use our pointing fingers to read the word we wrote.

"Who can show me on their fingers what word is next?" I call on a student and watch him break the sentence into words, using his fingers. "Yes, *light*. Is *light* a word we know and can just write, or do we have to listen carefully to the sounds? You're right. We haven't learned this word and it's not on the word wall, so we need to pull the sounds apart and count them on our fingers. Do it with me." I put up a fist. "*lll-iii-t*. We can hear three sounds. Back to our first finger. That sound was *lll*." The students call out that the letter *l* makes that sound. "Yep, sounds like an *l* to me. We don't need to check it in our picture alphabet book; let's just write an *l*. Don't forget a finger space. Lay your finger right next to the *e* and leave it there so you can see exactly where to put the *l*. We can't hook *l* onto the end of *the*! Start at the top." I circulate and check to see that everyone puts a space between the words. "Get your fingers up again for *light*. What's the second sound? I hear *iii*. That's easy—*i*. Now the last sound. Do it with me and listen carefully for the sound at the end: *lll-iii-t*." I call on a few students. "That's what I hear, too. Let's write it. Remember, lowercase *t* isn't quite as tall as the other tall letters. Okay, let's point and read and make sure our sentence is turning out the way we want it to. *The light . . .*" I tap the area right after the word *light* and students say, "*is*."

Similar steps are taken for the word *is*, treating it as a word the class knows. In other words, we don't segment the sounds; we just find the word on the word wall and copy it.

For the word *red,* the students break into a song they've just learned, "*R-e-d, red, r-e-d, red, I can spell red. . . .*" I remind them that they can also look at the color chart and copy the word since I have introduced the color chart as a resource and given them several instances to practice referring to it. I take the time to reiterate the proper letter formation as I write *red* and have the students watch me write each individual letter before allowing them to write the letters on their papers.

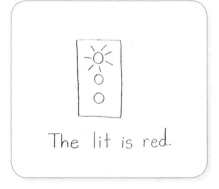

My completed drawing and sentence

When we are finished with the four words, we point to the words and read the sentence. "Does it sound good? Does it sound the way we wanted it to? Does it sound like we're finished? If we're finished with a sentence, what do we put at the end? Yes, a period. Make sure your period is a nice small dot, not a big hairball."

Creating Closure on Drawing and Writing

"I'm coming around to check your sentence. If it looks good and has a period, I'll give you a star." Since I have circulated and assisted students throughout the lesson to ensure that all students were keeping up and doing quality work, it does not take me long to determine that everyone's work is worthy of a star.

Justin, age 5 A student's picture and writing from this whole-group lesson shows excellent attention to shapes, spaces between words, and letter formation.

INSTRUCTIONAL CONCEPTS AND STRATEGIES TO SUPPORT WHOLE-GROUP WRITING LESSONS

The information in the previous section focused on structuring and managing the four main components of the whole-group drawing and writing lesson. Below, you will read about the most important instructional strategies to include in your lessons to support students as they move toward the goal of beginning to write more independently.

Two Ways to Write a Word

The first six weeks of writing instruction will allow you time to introduce and model the use of several basic sight words upon which students will rely when starting to write their own sentences. High-frequency words that kindergarten students will use in their writing, specifically words that cannot be sounded out, should be brought up and emphasized as words students need to learn and know. Certain key words, such as *a, the, I, see,* and *is* should not only be introduced but should be used repeatedly in the phrases or sentences you write during your direct-instructed writing lessons, as well as at other times during the school day. This is a good time to start a word list or word wall of frequently used words that students can refer to for their writing or reading needs throughout the school year. By the end of the first six weeks, I have posted on the word wall approximately six to eight words, such as *I, me, a, the, see,* and *is.* These are words I have introduced deliberately and referred to frequently. Students have used them often enough that we consider them *words we know.*

Explicitly teach students that there are two categories of words and thus two ways to write words:

1. If the word is a known word (i.e., it has been formally introduced and discussed), write the word from memory or by finding the word posted somewhere in the classroom.

2. If the spelling of the word is not known, listen to the sounds in the word and write as many letters as possible for those sounds.

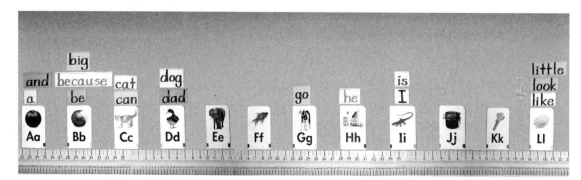

This word wall from a half-day kindergarten class during the month of December includes 34 sight words.

Guide students as they decide in which category a word belongs and then as they write the word: First, students should ask themselves, "Is this a word we know or is this a word whose sounds we should listen to?" If it is a word that has been formally introduced and taught and is displayed on the word wall or elsewhere in the room, then it is considered a word that has been learned or a *word we know*. Students either write the word from memory, find the word and copy it, or recall having been introduced to that word and understand what you mean when you prompt them to find and copy the word correctly.

Teach students that if the word is not known then they will need to use their fingers to listen to and count the sounds in the word. You will model this and walk them through this during the first six weeks of whole-group guided instruction. Later, when they start writing independently, reassure them that for words they don't know by sight, any letter or group of letters they choose to write is acceptable and correct, as long as they have tried hard to hear all the sounds and write the letters that match those sounds. Keep in mind that not all words need to be, nor should be, spelled correctly. You mostly want to see letters that go with the phonemes that can be heard.

Using a Word Wall to Reinforce High-Frequency Words

There are many different types of word walls, but a word wall that lists high-frequency words seems to be the most useful in a kindergarten classroom. I like to combine my word wall with the displayed picture alphabet, as shown below, so each letter, its picture, and some words that begin with that letter are all together in one place.

Not only will a word wall provide your students the opportunity to find words they know and copy them, but copying words time after time will assist students in learning them and eventually committing them to memory. Also, when students have at least a few words in their writing spelled conventionally, both you and they more easily will be able to read what they have written.

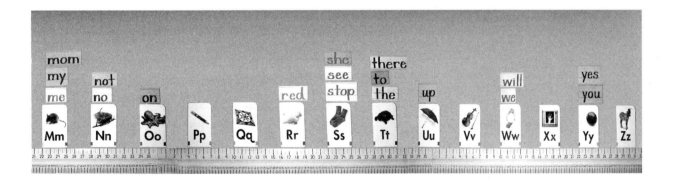

Words can be introduced to students as early as the first week of school. Some teachers feel that learning needs to happen sequentially and systematically; that is, first students should learn the names and sounds of the letters, next they should learn words, and only after knowing several sight words are they ready to learn to write and read. This process is next to impossible to control since students come to school today with very different backgrounds and different knowledge bases. It is also too time consuming (it can take months to introduce and teach the names of the letters if done one at a time) and limits students' learning and achievement. If students are encouraged to use any and all letters and sounds from the beginning, especially in an authentic learning situation such as daily writing, they will rapidly learn the names and sounds of the letters.

Not only can students begin writing when they know only a few letters, but the process of writing common words right away will help them quickly acquire additional letter names and sounds. When given opportunities to work with basic sight words like *the* and to learn how to locate them on the word wall, students will learn to recognize, read, and write the words, while at the same time learning the names of the letters needed to spell the words.

When to Add Words to the Word Wall

Words should be added to the word wall after you have formally introduced them to the students. For example, when teaching students the word *the*, incorporate a song, an activity or two, and several opportunities for students to use the word in both writing and reading before adding it to the word wall. All of these activities can happen on the same day and should not be spread out over too much time. The point is to help students see this group of letters as a distinct unit and to get the word on the word wall as soon as possible. To add a word to the word wall, students need to be present and watch you write the word and actually attach it to the word wall. This allows you to hold students accountable for knowing that it is there. Refer to the word wall often and plan activities that help students review and practice recognizing, reading, and writing the words that have been placed on it. Students usually enjoy keeping a running count of how many words have been added to the word wall and how many of these words they already know how to read and write.

CREATING BALANCE: WRITING WITH THE TWO TYPES OF WORDS

At any point in teaching young children to write, it is important to teach and expect a near equal use of known words and unknown words. When this balance is not in place, it will impede the class's overall progress. If students are not familiar with a handful of high-frequency words, then it will be difficult for them to write and difficult for anyone to read what they have written. On the other hand, if students are not comfortable with the process of attempting to listen to and segment sounds and then write the corresponding letters, they will struggle to write anything independently. There will always be a few students who find learning sight words very challenging, and there will always be a few students who do not enjoy taking the risk of writing unknown words. If, however, your class as a whole seems to need to sound everything out, or, on the other hand, seems to stick mainly with sight words, then the balance between these two types of words may go awry.

Once a word is on the word wall, most students should be expected to always spell the word correctly. Some students will already know the word, some will remember exactly where you placed it and will be able to find it on their own, others will need reminders about where to find it, and some may not yet fully understand the significance of grouping letters together. The expectation is that students will forevermore spell *the* correctly, but you will adjust this expectation accordingly for each of your students.

Choosing Words for the Word Wall

You should not necessarily teach only the words that appear on a typical official high-frequency word list, as shown on the next page, and they should not be introduced in the exact order in which they appear. For example, the words *mom, dad, cat, dog, love,* and the teacher's name will not appear on any standard list of high-frequency words but will most definitely be some of the most regularly used words in your students' writing and thus should be added to the class word wall at some point in the year. Words that are important but are not necessarily those that your students will use often in their journals, such as color and number words, should be displayed somewhere other than the high-frequency word wall and pointed out to students so they know how to access them. Adding too many words to the word wall will only clutter it and make it difficult for the students to use it as a resource.

In order for students to realize which words are on the word wall and to commit some of them to memory, words must be introduced slowly and steadily and students must have time to absorb them. Student writing such as Dean's, shown here, may tempt you to rush into teaching too many basic sight words, such as *like, play, you,* and *fun,* too soon. It works best, however, to determine in advance when and why certain sight words will be introduced to the class. Knowing that you have a plan will make it easier to force yourself to hold off on introducing too many words too quickly. A yearlong plan overview that lists which sight words are to be introduced to my half-day class and when is shown on page 37. Notice how I've tied certain sight words into the plan through our thematic units and shared reading titles.

The SNo is white. I lic to Pla in the SNo. I lic sNo
Pecas U can Pla in the SNo is Fon Pecas U can
ac a SNoMAN. I can Mac a Fort. I can Mac a SNo aShol.

Dean, age 6

First 100 High-Frequency Words

the	or	out	its
of	by	them	who
and	one	then	now
a	had	she	people
to	not	many	my
in	but	some	made
is	what	so	over
you	all	these	did
that	were	would	down
it	when	other	only
he	we	into	way
for	there	has	find
was	can	more	use
on	an	her	may
are	your	two	water
as	which	like	long
with	their	him	little
his	said	see	very
they	if	time	after
at	do	could	words
be	will	no	called
this	each	make	just
from	about	than	where
I	how	first	most
have	up	been	know

Yearlong Plan Overview

Date	Theme	Sight Words/Chunks
Aug. 20	Busy Bee, rules	*I*
Aug. 27	First names	*me*
Sept. 3	Birthdays	*a, red*
Sept. 10	Bus	*the, th, stop*
Sept. 17	Colors	*I, see,* color words
Sept. 24	Scarecrows	*is,* color words
Oct. 1	Safety	*is, stop, go, red, green, yellow*
Oct. 8	Apples	*up, like, red, green, yellow*
Oct. 15	Leaves	*is, can,* color words
Oct. 22	T-shirts	*he, she, me, we, look, sh*
Oct. 29	Halloween	*look, -at* words
Nov. 5	Voting, *Little Red Hen*	*little, yes, no, go, so*
Nov. 12	*Little Red Hen*	*little, not, will*
Nov. 19	Thanksgiving	*you*
Nov. 26	Family, houses	*mom, dad, little, my, will*
Dec. 3	Opposites	*yes, no, big, little, cat, dog, on, off, and*
Dec. 10	The Gingerbread Man	*can, -an* words, *my*
Dec. 17	Holiday (star)	*are, -ar* words, *to, from, there*
Jan. 7	New Year's, last names	
Jan. 14	Winter	blends (*sn* in *snow*)
Jan. 21	Martin Luther King, Jr.	*-ing,* blends (*bring, swing, sting*)
Jan. 28	Days of the week	*day, -ay* words, blends, *-s* ending
Feb. 4	100th Day of School	*day, -ay* words, *have, has, had*
Feb. 11	Valentine's Day, friends	*love, very, to, from*
Feb. 18	U.S.A.	*of (U.S. of A., Statue of Liberty, Pledge of Allegiance)*
Feb. 25	Questions, Dr. Seuss	*wh-* question words
Mar. 3	Ducks	*all, -all* words, number words
Mar. 17	Spring, eggs	*all, -all*
Mar. 24	Spring, wind, rain	
Mar. 31	Plants	
April 7	Caterpillars and butterflies	"ow brothers" (*ou, ow*)
April 14	Teeth	*too, -oo, -ed* ending
April 21	Earth Day, Earth's animals	*-oo*
April 28	Farm, baby animals	
May 5	Mother's Day	*-ay, -ot, got*
May 12	Watermelon	
May 19	Pizza	

Tip: Start introducing words slowly but steadily.

Tip: Introduce words more quickly now that students understand the concept of word and how to use the word wall. Emphasizing the same word over a span of several weeks is helpful. Also, students may be ready to work with small letter chunks and word families.

Tip: Continue to teach letter chunks and also introduce the idea of blends. Add words to the word wall that are significant to each specific class.

Tip: As the end of the year approaches, there will be less time for students to practice and learn new words. Begin to taper off the introduction and addition of words and focus more on letter chunks and spelling patterns.

As the months go on, notice the words that your students attempt to write often that you have not formally introduced during shared reading or another activity. When you feel it will be helpful but not too overwhelming, tell your students that you are going to add a certain word to the word wall because you have noticed that a lot of them are trying to use that word on a regular basis. A perfect example is the word *because*. *Because* is not a word that teachers expect kindergartners to be able to spell, and yet they attempt to write it often during independent writing, as shown in Adelynn's writing below. Therefore, it makes sense to explain to your students that you noticed they are using this word a lot and you are going to add it to the word wall so they can start spelling it correctly. Before you know it, you will have several kindergarten students who have memorized how to spell the word *because* and no longer need to refer to the word wall when trying to write it.

Kindergarten students thrive on analyzing and sorting words. As the year goes on, use this to your advantage to create other word lists, such as *wh-* question words, long words, words with unusual ("goofy") spellings, and rhyming word families. Post these word collections around the classroom in places other than the high-frequency word wall. As you would do with the words on the word wall, discuss these special words, create word cards for them, and post the cards together so the students know how and where to find them during writing time. But do not hold students accountable for spelling these words correctly. Some students will be developmentally ready to use these additional resources, but others will not and should not be expected to.

My Teeth are hELthey. bee Kus I Brush my teeth Evry nit AnD Evry day. Evn on Bthdays.

Adelynn, age 5

Sound Segmentation

Model on several occasions each day how to separate the sounds in words. A useful technique for teaching this skill, and one that students can begin to use on their own even early in the school year, is to count the phonemes in short words. Put up one finger as the first sound is elongated, a second finger for the next phoneme, and so forth, in the same sequence that you would raise your fingers to count and show numbers, as shown in the phoneme segmentation examples on page 24. Once a word has been completely stretched out, students can check your fingers or their own fingers to determine how many letters they should try to write to represent that word.

This technique is similar to Vygotsky's materialization, in which a tangible object or physical action is used to represent each heard sound (Galperin, 1992). Students' ability to use this technique will gradually improve as the school year progresses. At no point is it necessary for students to be at the same ability level or to separate and count the sounds in all words perfectly; the purpose in teaching them this technique is to give them the means of separating sounds in order to get letters down on paper when they are writing independently.

Using Classroom Alphabets to Teach Sound-Symbol Relationships

The following sequence of activities, to be done outside of daily writing time, will help students make the most of the alphabets in the classroom. (Helpful information about choosing a classroom alphabet is found in the materials preparation section on page 17.)

- First, sing the traditional alphabet song (to the tune of "Twinkle, Twinkle Little Star") without directing the students' attention to a posted alphabet. Be sure they are familiar with the song and can enunciate most of the letters in the song. Most likely, some will not separate the letters in the *l, m, n, o, p* section at this point; if not, it is okay to move on.

- Next, begin to point to each letter in the alphabet as you and the students sing the song more slowly. Students will begin to associate the letter names to the symbols, as well as practice one-to-one correspondence and voice-print match, which may be difficult tasks for many this early in the year but should be practiced anyway. Continue modeling how to point to each letter in sequence, emphasizing that only one letter name should be said for each letter that is touched. It is helpful to break the song into its natural phrases and do only one portion at a time. Begin with *a, b, c, d, e, f, g,* singing and touching each letter as the students watch.

- Have a few students stand before the class and try the above activity, assisting them when they have trouble with one-to-one correspondence.

- Move the class on to other portions of the alphabet, even if not all students have mastered the first section. It will be several months into the school year before most students can do this accurately, but they need opportunities to begin practicing now.

- Take the time to point out all the alphabets in the classroom. Tell students that any of these can be used as a resource when writing.

- Create a picture-alphabet big book, purchase a picture-alphabet chart, or enlarge the one on page 62 for your daily review. Teach a chant that helps students acquire the letter names and sounds and to connect each letter to at least one word that begins with its sound. The chant should include saying the name of the letter, the letter's sound, and the name of the picture for that letter. For example, when you point to *Cc,* you might say, "Capital *C,* lowercase *c,* /k/-/k/, cat." Work on a set of five or fewer letters at a time and repeat this set of letters two or three times in one sitting.

Once students have settled into the routine of daily writing and you no longer have to spend as much time on management and getting names on papers, begin modeling how to use a picture alphabet as one of the strategies used to determine which letter to write for a sound that is heard. Using a picture alphabet is a vital skill for students who often find themselves in the predicament of being able to hear a phoneme but not knowing which letter to write for that sound.

After stretching the sounds in the label you and your students are going to write, draw the students' attention back to the first sound by putting up just your index finger. Ask them to listen carefully while you say the first sound again. Then ask what letter they think it sounds like. Some students will have no idea and others will inform you before you even ask. To honor everyone, show how students can use the picture alphabet to find out which letter they need or how they can use the picture alphabet to check to see if they are right. For example, if you are writing *sun* with your students, drag out the /s/ sound, and once a student has suggested the letter *s,* find *s* and its picture in the alphabet and say, "Does *ssssun* sound like *sssssandwich*? Yes, it does, so *s* must be the letter we need." You can see how this is embedded within a lesson in the mid-August and late-September sample lessons.

Phonemic awareness (the ability to hear and isolate phonemes) in words that have two or three sounds is a skill that seems to come fairly quickly for most students. The next step, determining which letter corresponds to a heard sound and how to actually write that letter (the phonics application) is where many students will encounter some difficulty in proceeding with their writing. For example, in attempting to write the word *fish* a student may say, "/F/, what makes the /f/ sound?" Or, if he knows that *f* makes the /f/ sound, he may wonder, "What does an *f* look like?" It is necessary, therefore, in the first six weeks to introduce, demonstrate, and let students practice finding the letter that goes with a particular sound, as discussed below.

Alphabet Teaching Tips

For the first situation above, where the student does not know what letter goes with the /f/ sound, or which symbol to write for most of the phonemes he isolates, it is imperative to teach the technique of using a picture alphabet to 1) find a picture that begins with the same sound and 2) copy the letter that corresponds to that picture. With the second scenario, where the student grasps that *f* is the letter that makes the /f/ sound but is not sure what a letter *f* looks like, the student should learn how to sing the alphabet song while pointing to the letters. The student will slowly touch each letter of the alphabet in order as he sings the song, until he arrives at the letter for which he is searching, which in this case is *f*. The student can then copy that letter onto his paper.

In addition to using a picture alphabet to determine which letters go with which sounds, demonstrate other strategies for determining sound-letter correspondence, such as how to:

- look at or think about pictures or objects that begin with the same sound
- match the sound you hear with the first sound in a classmate's name and then check that student's name card for the right letter
- match the sound with a sight word that has been introduced and is posted
- think about what your mouth is doing with a particular sound ("Remember, if your lips are together, you're making an *m*.")

BUT THAT'S NOT HOW YOU SPELL IT!

There may be a student or two in class who brings to your attention that you really *do* know how to spell words and that you are not spelling them correctly. If this happens, gently remind the student that for now you are showing everyone how to write the sounds that you hear, which is the first step in learning to write words. You may want to tell students that if they already know how to spell a word they can go ahead and spell it on their papers but they also need to copy what you have written, so they can practice the sounds they hear. This shows respect for their desire to do it correctly while also downplaying any implication that the other students (or you) do not know the correct spelling.

Keep in mind that the ability to separate sounds into words and determine how many sounds are in a given word will vary greatly from student to student. Likewise, knowing which letters to use to represent the sounds heard and how to form the letters develops at different rates among students. Some students will pick up on some or all of these skills immediately while others will still be struggling with them at the end of the school year. It is important, however, to introduce the process of listening, separating, and counting sounds and recording letters for those sounds right at the beginning of the school year, because students will rely upon your modeling and their practice of this process when it comes time to do it on their own.

Establishing a Base of Known Letters

Students will feel more confident with writing once they establish a base of known letters. To start this process, have each student learn the names of the letters in his or her first name. Each day as they write their names on their daily writing papers, circulate among students and speak to them briefly about how they are writing their names. You can indirectly teach the letters in their names just by mentioning them and talking about them ("Look, Taylor, the *T* at the beginning of your name is a tall letter"); however, it is also helpful to periodically quiz students about the names of the letters in their first names and then take the time to explicitly teach one or two of them. When you stop at Taylor's seat, for example, ask her to tell you the letters she has written for her name. Encourage her to move from left to right. If she can tell you the names of most of the letters, in order, then ask her to name them out of sequence. When she can tell you a letter name consistently, put a line under that letter on the name card she is using as an example from which to copy. This will serve as a permanent record of which letter names have been mastered and which have not. Soon, students will want to get a line under each letter in their names and so will be motivated to learn the names of the remaining letters.

Do not be concerned that this activity will result in each student having a different knowledge base of letter names. Even if a letter-of-the-week format is used to introduce and teach the names of the letters, teachers cannot really control how many letters and which letters each student knows at any given point in time. Some come to school knowing them all, some will pick up on letter names before they are formally introduced, and some will struggle with learning them even if they are taught sequentially in a strategic order.

Encouraging Spacing Between Words

It will be necessary to introduce the idea of spacing between words when you begin to write two-word phrases with your students. Remind students regularly that a space is used to show where one word ends and another begins and that people cannot read writing unless there are spaces between the words. A good tool for spacing—something that is always with a student and is the perfect size—is an index finger. Model how to make a "finger space" by placing the index finger opposite your writing hand in front of each new word you write. You can see how to incorporate using finger spacing in the late-September lesson. As you circulate about the room during these lessons, support students in trying finger spacing and encouraging them to follow your model on the overhead.

Most students' ability to space between words will develop concurrently with their ability to record sounds for words. For the few students who will struggle with spacing, refer to the individualized mini-lessons on page 132.

Establishing the Expectation for Correct Letter Formation

While the importance of proper letter formation and neat handwriting has waned over the past few decades since the introduction of computers and word processing into our culture, it is vital that these skills do not get shortchanged in kindergarten and first-grade classrooms. Clear, neat handwriting in and of itself is not necessarily crucial in today's world, but it can significantly influence a student's self-esteem, confidence, spelling and reading skills, and the substance of present and future interactions with teachers, parents, and peers. When students' writing is exceptionally neat in appearance, others take note and make positive comments about it, and if it is at least adequate, it may keep students from having to redo sloppy schoolwork for years to come. If improper letter formation or letter height is condoned, careless handwriting will quickly become a bad habit. The habit will be hard to break, and students will likely resign themselves to the notion that neat handwriting and quality work are not attainable goals for them.

The best teaching strategy for helping your students acquire nice handwriting is for sloppy or improper handwriting never to be an option and, therefore, never develop. There will always be some kindergartners for whom beautiful handwriting is just not a timely focus, but expect the majority of your students to use their best handwriting at all times. Remember, poor handwriting is, in most cases, just a habit and, as with most bad habits, it is much wiser to prevent it than to try to break it later.

There is so much to introduce and include in the whole-group guided writing lessons during the first six weeks of school that it might be tempting to omit handwriting instruction for now and to plan to start it up at some point in the future. Avoid this mistake: You will save yourself a lot of time and energy if you start modeling and expecting correct letter formation from day one.

Teaching Tips for Letter Formation

Letters can be categorized into three main groups—tall letters, short letters, and letters that hang down. Decide ahead of time if you will use these or other terms for the different types of letters and then use your terms consistently throughout the school year. Something else to think about before beginning handwriting instruction is how exactly you want students to form letters. Come up with a quick prompt or set of directions for each letter (see the Letter Formation Cues at right) and repeat them over and over again when modeling writing. For the most part, reiterate to students that most letters are formed by starting at the top and not lifting the pencil unless absolutely necessary. Also, the majority of letters you model and talk about should be lowercase since this is what we want students to use.

Expect and allow students to say the cues aloud while they form letters. The process of saying aloud the letter formation cues not only ensures the development of functional and legible handwriting that will not need to be retaught in later grades, but also assists students in being able to visualize letters and more easily remember their names. You may hear students repeating the cues in many instances as an aid for remembering letter names. Most students will need the entire school year to master the proper formation of all the letters.

Letter Formation Cues for Lowercase Letters

The cues listed below serve as short prompts or reminders for students. Use them as they are or tailor them to match your teaching style, curriculum, and student needs. Encourage students to verbalize the cues as they form letters, especially those letters that are difficult to make or often turn out reversed.

a	Make a *c*, up, down
b	Start at the top, straight down, circle around
c	Curve up and around and touch the ground
d	Make a *c*, go all the way up, and trace it down
e	Straight across and around
f	Curve up and around, down, and cross it
g	Make a *c*, go up, trace it down, down with a hook
h	Start at the top, go down, trace it up with a bump
i	Straight down, dot in the sky
j	Straight down, down with a hook, dot in the sky
k	Start at the top, straight down, little sideways *v* at the bottom
l	Start at the top, straight down to the ground
m	Go down, trace it up, bump, bump
n	Go down, trace it up, bump
o	Start at the top, circle back, close it perfectly
p	Straight down, down, trace it up, and circle around
q	Make a *c*, go up, straight down, down with a tail
r	Go down, trace it up with a curve
s	Forward *c*, backward *c*

Tip: Since the formation of many letters begins with the letter *c*, teach the letter *c* as early as possible.

Tip: Having students start at the *top* rather than the *sky line* works with both unlined and lined paper, whereas starting at the *sky line* might be confusing on unlined paper.

Tip: Having students make a *c* first helps prevent *b* and *d* reversals. Be sure students understand that *trace* means to go over part of a line that was already made.

Tip: Mentioning the *little* sideways *v* will prevent lowercase *k* from turning out to be a capital *K*.

Tip: Although lowercase *o* does not start at the top (as in where the skyline is), reminding students to start up high thwarts the action of starting *o* at the bottom and circling forward.

t	Start at the top, go down, and cross it
u	Go down, curve it up, trace it down
v	Diagonal down, diagonal up
w	Diagonal down, up, down, up
x	Diagonal down, diagonal down
y	Short diagonal, long diagonal
z	Forward, diagonal back, forward again

Tip: Point out to students that although *t* is a tall letter, it is not as tall as the other tall letters. You may want to refer to it as "teenager *t.*"

Tip: Teach students what *diagonal* means.

Tip: Repeatedly remind students that the short diagonal needs to go down low, not up at the top.

Tip: Use the terms *capital* and *uppercase* interchangeably.

Letter Formation Cues for Capital Letters

Follow the relevant tips given in the lowercase letter formation cues chart, as well as the new ones mentioned here.

A	Start at the top, diagonal down, diagonal down, cross it
B	Start at the top, go down, hop to the top, bump, bump
C	Curve up and around and touch the ground
D	Start at the top, go down, hop to the top, big bump
E	Start at the top, go down, hop to the top, stick, stick, stick
F	Start at the top, go down, hop to the top, stick, stick
G	Make a *C*, cut in
H	Start at the top, down, down, across
I	Start at the top, straight down, across the top, across the bottom

Tip: Though it may seem easier to start at the bottom to make capital *A*, it is important to be consistent with starting letters at the top.

Tip: Show students that they have to lift their pencils to *hop to the top*.

Tip: Since students write capital *I* so frequently, you will have many opportunities to remind them to make all three lines as straight as they can.

J	Start at the top, down with a hook, across the top
K	Start at the top, straight down, big sideways *V*
L	Start at the top, straight down and across
M	Start at the top, straight down, hop to the top, down, up, down
N	Start at the top, straight down, hop to the top, down, up
O	Start at the top, circle back, close it perfectly
P	Start at the top, straight down, hop to the top, one bump
Q	Start at the top, circle back, close it perfectly, add a tail
R	Start at the top, straight down, hop to the top, one bump, diagonal down
S	Start at the top, forward *c*, backward *c*
T	Start at the top, straight down, across the top
U	Start at the top, go down, curve it up
V	Start at the top, diagonal down, diagonal up
W	Start at the top, diagonal down, up, down, up
X	Start at the top, diagonal down, diagonal down
Y	A little *v* up high, straight line down
Z	Start at the top, forward, diagonal back, forward again

Tip: Remind students that capital *M* has points; lowercase *m* has bumps.

The main goal of writing instruction is to get kids writing. Once they are able to get several letters on their papers, you can, and should, start the process of refining their handwriting. Be assured that after six weeks of modeled writing, during which you've explicitly taught letter formation, and six weeks of intense instruction in helping students write their first names, most students will attend to their handwriting with care and have surprisingly neat print when they start writing independently in October. In addition, try to make time outside of daily journal writing time for direct instruction and practice in letter formation and handwriting (see page 151 for ideas). Establish a common language base with your students for referring to certain types of letters and for the correct formation of letters and expect students to apply this information anytime they are required to write.

Establishing Functional Pencil Grasps

A priority for kindergarten teachers should be aiding students in developing a proper pencil grasp for handwriting tasks. An efficient pencil grasp uses muscles that are capable of precision and speed and lessens fatigue. Once again, because of the adaptable nature of this age group and the opportunity you have to help students learn lifelong habits, do what you can to establish a proper pencil grasp for each student now because by first grade it may be too difficult to change a grasp.

The optimal pencil grasp, shown in the figure below, is known as the tripod grasp, where the pencil is supported by the thumb, index finger and middle finger. Ideally, the pencil should rest upon the middle finger. The ring and little fingers curl in toward the palm of the hand, with the little finger and the side of the hand and wrist resting on the table while writing.

One of the most common variations of the tripod grasp that you will see in kindergarten students is the four finger grasp. This is when a student uses the ring finger, and sometimes the little finger as well, to grip the pencil. Grasping the pencil in this way usually causes the fingers to straighten too much and the hand to lift off the table when writing. Another common adaptation is for students to increase stability for the pencil by squeezing the top of the thumb close to the index finger, so the pencil presses more tightly against the webbing between the thumb and the index finger. This grasp is easy to recognize because the student's thumb will be pointing forward or straight up. While students may feel the pencil is more stable this way, their inability to use their thumb to push the pencil ultimately results in less control. Moreover, a thumb that isn't on the pencil tends to stick out, making it difficult for students to see the tip and therefore view their marks as they write.

It is difficult to watch constantly for correct pencil grasps in a classroom full of students. To make this less overwhelming, assess students' pencil grasps as soon as possible and group them into one of the following categories. Corrective cues for each grasp are provided.

Observations	Corrective Cues
Student consistently demonstrates the correct tripod grasp and has no immediate needs.	None needed.
Student has a four-finger grip.	*Tuck in pinky and/or ring finger.*
Student's thumb is not on the pencil.	*Get your thumb on your pencil.*
Student has the middle finger on top of the pencil, using it to drive the pencil.	*Middle finger goes under the pencil. It's a chair for the pencil to sit on.*
Student tends to hold the pencil vertically.	*Lean your pencil back* (i.e., into the webbing between the index finger and thumb).
Student holds the pencil too high or too low.	*Hold your pencil where the paint part starts and the wood part ends.*
Student has not established a dominant hand.	Determine, as soon as possible, whether the right or left hand is going to provide the most control and then provide reminders to use the dominant hand, when necessary, such as: *Switch to your writing hand.*
Student has other pencil grasp issues that may require collaboration with a special needs teacher.	

You can use the chart on page 56 to categorize your students.

When you have the opportunity, pick up a pencil and model for those students who need it what a correct pencil grasp looks like. Help them get their fingers on their pencils just as you have yours on the pencil you are holding. Point out to each student what it is that he or she needs to change. Develop some short phrases, such as the corrective cues listed above, that you can use as reminders for students who need to shift their grasps. A new pencil grasp may feel awkward to students and some will resist your attempts at changing their grasps. Talk to them about why you want to help them make this change, that holding a pencil correctly will help them write more neatly and faster and that our hands do not get as tired when we hold our pencils correctly. Also, explain that they will better be able to see what they are writing.

Enlist the support of parents by sending home a picture of the desired pencil grasp and by letting them know in what area their child may need support. Inform them that if they provide reminders at home about holding a pencil correctly the process of improving their child's pencil grasp will go much faster. (You'll find a reproducible sample letter on the next page.)

Name _____

Pencil Grasp

One of the skills we work on in kindergarten is a correct pencil grasp. Like most things, if a correct grasp is not developed at a young age, then it becomes more and more difficult to change. The recommened grasp is the tripod grasp, shown below:

TRIPOD

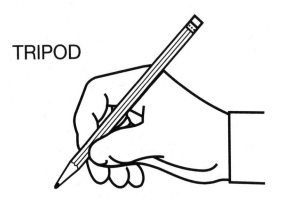

_____ Your child is consistently using a tripod pencil grasp, or other acceptable grasp.

_____ Your child needs reminders to hold a pencil correctly. Please help out with this at home.

Preparing Students to Write Independently

As you start daily writing instruction at the beginning of the school year, keep in mind the goal of having students write independently in approximately six weeks. Consider the procedural knowledge and skills they will need in order to transition to a block of writing time that is not teacher-directed and address these competencies in your whole-group direct instruction during the first six weeks. For any procedures you establish, make sure the majority of your students actually understand them and consider them each day. With skills, it is different; students should be made aware of them through your modeling, but do not expect mastery at this time. Points to emphasize often, in preparation for October when you will no longer be standing before the class providing direct instruction, are:

- Know and think about the topic that has been given for the day.

- Draw a picture first. Put the drawing at the bottom of the paper.

- Draw as well as you can and do not worry if the picture on your paper does not match exactly the picture you have in your mind.

- Add details to help others understand what it is you are trying to draw.

- Do not spend too much time drawing; you will need time to write letters and words.

- Think of some words to write that go with the picture.

- Count how many words you are going to write.

- Think about the first word; determine if it is a word you already know or if it is a word for which you are going to try and listen to the sounds.

- Write the word, or write the letters for as many of the sounds as you can hear.

- If you know a place in the classroom where you can find out how to write the entire word or one of the letters that makes a sound you hear, take the time to find it and copy it, even if you have to get out of your chair.

- If you are not sure about a word or a sound, try your hardest and then move on.

- When you finish the first word, use a finger space to show that you are starting a new word.

- Write the rest of the words in your sentence, using as many sounds and letters as you know and putting a finger space between the words.

- When you are all done, put a period at the end of your sentence.

- Touch each word you write with your finger and read your writing to see if it sounds right to you.

- If writing time is not yet over, add some details to your picture or write some more words to go with your picture.

Modeling how and teaching students to verbally rehearse what they are planning on writing will improve their ability to write a coherent thought. For a one-word label, students should have modeled for them how to hear, separate, and determine approximately how many sounds are in the word. They may not be able to conclude the exact number of sounds in a word, which letters represent the sounds they can hear, or even how to write those letters; however, they should know enough about these processes to at least feel competent in getting started when it comes to writing a label independently. Likewise, if they are ready to write a sentence, students should have witnessed plenty of modeling on how to think of sentences that correspond with their pictures, how to count the number of words in their sentences, and how to write one or more sounds per word. As you circulate among your students in the months to come, you will model repeatedly, to individual students, how to count the sounds in words or how to write a sentence, but you will never again have the opportunity to teach these skills from scratch in the highly organized, well-thought-out lessons you are providing at this time. Therefore, be sure to take advantage of these six weeks of direct instruction to model these skills often.

TEACHING BEHAVIORS CONDUCIVE TO LEARNING

As you teach content, you will want your students to understand how their behavior can influence their learning. The following are key elements you want to cultivate from day one.

Engaging in Instruction

One of the advantages of whole-group instruction during the first six weeks of school is that it presents the perfect opportunity to teach children how to engage in instruction. Relentlessly insist that students look at the overhead every time you are about to model something that they will copy. Teach them to think actively about what you are saying whenever you are teaching by suggesting some thoughts that should be going on in their heads at any particular moment. For example, if you have just demonstrated how to make a lowercase *g* on the overhead, you could say, "You probably noticed and you're probably thinking that lowercase *g* is kind of like lowercase *a* and kind of like lowercase *d* because we start all of these letters the same way. When we write them, we make a *c* first and then we finish the letter." Also, encourage students to raise their hands and participate as often as possible. And teach them that when it is not their turn to answer a question or do something in front of the class, they can still take a turn in their heads. They can think about what they would say or how they would do it if the teacher called on them.

As the weeks go on, the need to request your students' attention will greatly diminish; they will not only be learning quickly how to attend and be engaged at school but they will also be so enthusiastic about drawing and writing that most really will not chance missing a single part of your instruction. The ability to listen and attend to instruction is not just a vital school skill you are developing in your students. It is also a good habit that will serve them well in many situations throughout their lives.

Working up to One's Potential

In addition to being engaged, students must learn the importance and the technique of always working up to their individual potential. In order to assist students with this, you need to be cognizant of exactly what each student is currently capable of doing. For example, if Reba is able to form a lowercase *e* on her own one day while writing her name, the new expectation for her is to always use a lowercase *e* and form it as well as or better than she did the day she discovered she could do it. It may be necessary to remind Reba that she now knows how to do it and it may even be necessary to assist her in performing that same skill again. The important thing is to make her feel as if she is working up to her ability by not allowing her the opportunity to go back to her old ways or to regress, even slightly, for one day. In other words, do not permit her to use a capital *E*, to go back to tracing the lowercase *e*, or to ask you to make it for her.

Most teachers rely on student observation and memory to keep track of students' current abilities and what to expect from them. The more you circulate around the room and watch students during each step of their learning, the more aware you will be of what each of them can and cannot do. A mental checklist you keep of each student will guide you in your scaffolding each day. Some teachers like to record what students have demonstrated so they have a written record to refer to. Either way, continually update the current abilities of each student so you can adjust your expectations accordingly.

COMMUNICATING WITH PARENTS

With this approach to teaching writing, you have a built-in system for communicating with parents, from the first week of school to the last, about what is happening in the classroom with writing instruction and how their children are progressing.

Written Comments

Because students write on individual sheets of paper for the first six weeks, instead of in journals, you will be able to send their work home frequently, even on a daily basis if you so desire. Take a few minutes to write a personal comment on each student's paper. This is crucial at the beginning of the year as it trains parents and students to really look at and discuss together work that is sent home.

When writing comments on students' papers, address the student directly, as if you were starting a letter: "Stanley, you put all your letters in a row instead of spreading them out all over the paper. Way to go!" Comments can also reflect any action you want a student to take. For example, you might write, "You have good sounds in your writing. Point to the word you wrote and read it to your family."

In other cases, you might address the parents, providing them with a tip for supporting their child, such as, "Please have Anna practice lowercase *a* at home. She gets frustrated when she tries and then it doesn't turn out looking like an *a*. Remind her to start with a letter *c* and then go up and back down." A note such as this makes it easier for parents to work with their children. First, it is specific; it tells the parent exactly what to have their child work on. It is also an extension of the individualized instruction that was delivered to that student that day, meaning that it is a fully customized homework assignment. You are telling Anna to start lowercase *a* by making a *c* and now her parents can tell her the same thing. And last, the note is from the teacher, which means the child will realize that it is you, not the parent, who is requesting that she practice a little at home. This may alleviate any power struggles that arise from parents asking their children to practice skills that are difficult for them.

Thoughtful comments will serve the purpose of helping you develop a rich relationship with your students; motivate parents and students to get school work home safely and take the time to review and discuss it; and serve as a means for communicating the intricacies of writing—how these are being presented in the classroom and what you are expecting students to do with them. It is imperative to send student writing home on a regular basis, even if your circumstances prevent you from finding time for daily written comments. To keep a student's writing in a journal that remains at school is not fair to parents or students. Kindergarten drawings and emergent writing are so delightful. Your students and their families have the right to share and to celebrate these first endeavors into the world of written language at the exact time that they are fresh and exciting.

Back-to-School Night

You may have the opportunity to speak to your students' parents as a group either at Back-to-School Night or at a Classroom and Curriculum Information Night early in the school year. The structure and timing your school uses for such events will determine to what degree you will be able to discuss the writing program in your classroom. If the opportunity to speak to parents happens very early on in the school year, or even before school starts, you may want to keep your information about the writing program to a minimum and save most of it for the fall parent-teacher conferences.

The most important message to convey to parents at the very beginning of the school year is that kindergarten is different than it was when they were in school (this is true for even the youngest of the parents) and that reading and writing instruction now begins in kindergarten. Assure parents that this is appropriate for kindergartners. Provide some information about your classroom and your teaching that will calm any parents who are feeling anxious about a reading and writing kindergarten classroom and will reassure parents who are absolutely hoping and expecting that this type of instruction takes place at this grade level.

Some parents may be apprehensive because their children do not yet know the names of the letters; they may assume that if you are going to be teaching reading and writing, then perhaps most students already know the letter names and you might not take the time to teach them. Explain that it is through learning to read and write that students will learn the names and sounds of the letters. For example, when you teach the word *the* you help students learn to read it, write it, and spell it. That means they not only learn to recognize the word *the*, but they also learn the letters *t*, *h*, and *e* needed to write the word. A single example like this is usually sufficient information for parents for the first few weeks of school. You will have plenty of opportunities in the future to explain the development of writing skills in young children to parents.

The question of phonics might arise when you are speaking to parents early in the school year. Do you teach phonics? You bet you do! It is impossible to teach writing in this manner without teaching phonics. And not only do you teach phonics, but you teach students how to apply their phonological knowledge to the process of writing. For parents who feel their children are ahead of the game, let them know that in a few short weeks you will have them engaged in independent journal writing that will allow students to work at their own instructional levels, with no ceiling of opportunity for any student. You may choose not to go into too much detail at this point because many parents are still focusing on the logistics of kindergarten, such as transportation, safety precautions that are in place at school, lunch procedures, and just getting to know you as their child's teacher for the year.

SHARING WHAT WORKS

The most important thing for parents to understand at this point about writing development is that children will benefit most from experimenting with writing sounds they hear rather than copying adult writing.

SKILLS ASSESSMENT

There are three major skills to focus on and assess during the first six weeks of school, including:

- correctly writing one's first name

- naming the letters in one's first name

- displaying, at least when prompted, an acceptable pencil grasp

It works well to assess these skills at about the third week of school, determine which students have not mastered one or more of the skills, and then zero in on those students and their areas of weakness for the next three weeks.

Writing One's First Name

Writing first names legibly is a common expectation for kindergarten students. Consider, however, the power of your expectation. If you expect students to write their first names perfectly, like your model, rather than just legibly, most students, with enough guidance and practice, will learn to write it very nicely. And for those who cannot and may never be able to write their names perfectly, your expectation will result in them writing it much better than they may have otherwise. Moreover, such an expectation at this point will result in neater handwriting throughout the year as well as an overall heightened quality of work in general.

With all the focused work on name writing the first six weeks of school, it is not unreasonable to think that most students will be able to write their names with near perfection at the end of six weeks. To assess which of your students can and cannot legibly write their name is fairly simple. First, you must establish your criteria for proficiency, which for most teachers would be:

- a capital letter at the beginning followed by lowercase letters

- legible handwriting

- correct letter height

The correct formation of all letters (e.g., starting at the top, lifting the pencil at the correct time, and so forth) should not be expected at this point because you will not have had adequate time to teach letter formation.

Keep a class list handy, or use the form provided on the next page, to track those students who are able to write their names according to the listed criteria and without referring to their name cards. A checkmark in each of the three middle columns on the chart provided indicates proficiency. Specific letters that need attention can be listed in the column on the right and referred to when you have the opportunity to individualize and focus your instruction on the areas that need improvement. As the first few weeks pass and you check off these skills for more students on your list, you will be increasingly narrowing the list of students for whom you need to provide additional name-writing support.

> **SUPPORT FOR NAME WRITING**
>
> It is possible to get nearly all of your students to write their names quite nicely. They will not continue to do this, however, unless you hold them accountable for it. In my classroom, students do not turn anything in without me glancing at it first. Looking at their names—and asking them to make changes, if necessary—is part of this process.

Name-Writing Assessment

Student	Capital, followed by lowercase	Legible handwriting	Correct letter height	Letters that need improvement

Naming Letters in One's First Name

As mentioned earlier, students will feel more confident during writing time once they know the names of at least a few letters. Learning the letters in their first names is a great place to start. You can keep an ongoing record of which letters in his or her name a student knows by underlining those letters on the student's name card or by recording such information on a separate data form. The name card approach affords students the opportunity to see a daily record of the letter names they know and will increase their motivation to learn the remaining letters. Also, if you record your assessment data on the student name cards then you do not need to carry a separate piece of paper or clipboard as you circulate around the room during daily writing time. Again, as the weeks go on, it will become apparent which students are going to need extra help learning the names of the letters in their names; you can then devote an extra minute here and there, whether it be during writing time, whole-group time, center-time instruction, or in notes to parents to elicit their help in teaching these letter names.

Pencil Grasp

Categorizing your students' pencil grasps on the chart shown on the next page is the first step of the tricky task of correcting grasps. Being familiar with students' pencil grasp tendencies will help you focus on improving this skill during writing time and throughout the day, and remind you to cue students to change their grasps, if need be.

Here are two problematic pencil grasps: These grasps block students' view of the pencil tip, a view which would help them control the pencil much better. Pencil grasps usually improve dramatically once you explain to students that they need to be able to see the tip of the pencil in order to write as neatly as they can.

Categories and Corrective Cues for Student Pencil Grasps

Students	Consistent and correct tripod grasp	Four finger grip ("Tuck pinky and ring finger under.")	Thumb is not on pencil ("Get your thumb on the pencil.")	Middle finger on top ("Middle finger goes under the pencil.")	Pencil is too vertical ("Lean your pencil back.")	Grasp too high or too low ("Hold the pencil where the paint starts.")	Dominant hand not established or other situation

Be steadfast in your efforts to ensure that all students meet the goals of writing their names correctly, naming the letters in their first names, and using a correct pencil grasp. Of course, some students will not master these skills within the first six weeks of school, so these skills will continue to be an instructional focus for them, even as you move the class forward with more advanced skills.

IN REVIEW: THE FIRST SIX WEEKS

In addition to writing their names, naming the letters in their names, and holding their pencils correctly, within this short six-week period your students will have developed an understanding of many of the basic concepts of print and the thought processes and skills required for this activity we call writing. Imagine a student entering kindergarten not knowing how to write his or her name and having had minimal opportunities or encouragement to draw or write and then, in a few short weeks, writing his or her name correctly and drawing and labeling pictures. Tremendous growth, especially in students seeing themselves as artists and writers, will most definitely take place during these first six weeks of school.

Parents, too, will notice that their children are already learning to write. As you send their daily writing papers home, they will see that their children's drawings have improved and that although they have copied the written portion of their work from the overhead they are indeed quickly developing writing competencies such as directionality, letter-name and letter-sound correspondence, and the understanding that their writing contains a message that they helped formulate and are able to read.

Again, the purpose for everything you introduce and model during these initial six weeks is to prepare students to work independently during daily writing time beginning in October. You will introduce almost every skill your students will need for writing throughout the year. You will demonstrate these skills, talk about them, and have your students try them in a guided practice format. But you will not expect your students to actually generalize and apply most of these skills until later in the school year. If you truly believe that your students can participate in drawing pictures and writing sentences with you this early in the school year and you are committed to incorporating 25 to 30 minutes of direct instruction for writing time each school day, you will observe that the majority of your students have acquired the necessary skills to successfully transition into independent writing after about six weeks.

Chapter Three

Independent Journal Writing: October–January

This portion of the yearlong plan may, at first glance, look familiar to you because of its more traditional journal-writing format. As you read on, however, you will discover several essential elements unique to this approach that will move kindergartners faster and further along the continuum of learning to write. Based on the yearlong plan shown on page 9, writing instruction during the next four months of school will entail:

- Introducing independent writing, during which students write in their own journals.

- Providing a daily writing topic.

- Teaching mainly through brief, individualized mini-lessons.

- Supporting students as they write at their instructional level and progress at their own rate, challenging them as they are ready, with no ceiling of opportunity.

- Bringing concrete closure to each student's daily writing; writing does not carry over to subsequent days.

DAILY WRITING TIME

You may sense before the end of the first six weeks of school that your students are ready to transition into independent writing, and you, too, may be eager to let them experience this next step. Try, however, for the full six weeks to continue with the whole-group instruction described in Chapter 2. This structured teaching you do—modeling how to draw simple pictures, listen to and separate sounds, and write letters, words, and sentences—will result in a much more successful first few weeks of independent writing as well as lay the foundation for students to develop advanced writing skills by end of the year. Furthermore, the move to independent writing will mean the end of direct instruction in drawing, and your students will miss it.

Amelia, age 5

As you transition into this phase of the yearlong plan, it makes sense to continue using the same block of time you have already established for daily writing. The students are trained to be very focused during this time period and are ready to write. And you are probably enjoying immensely this peaceful yet purposeful learning time that has been established for writing.

MATERIALS PREPARATION: JOURNALS

Before beginning independent writing, you will need to prepare a journal for each student. A journal is basically a limited number of papers bound together into a booklet in which a student will draw and write. The best journals you can prepare for your students are ones that meet your needs as well as your students'. To begin with, create one journal type that is reasonably appropriate for all students in your class so that you can discuss procedures and expectations without confusion. Different types of journals that support different student needs can be introduced as needed once students have transitioned to writing independently.

To make the easiest, most economical, and effective style of journal, fasten eight to twelve plain, unlined pieces of paper together with a cover sheet. The staple should be placed so that the top and bottom edges of the journal are 11 inches and the sides are 8 ½ inches. This landscape orientation allows students a longer area in which to write before they need to execute a return sweep. If students perceive the paper as narrow, they may be more inclined to return sweep after every word or two they write. On the cover sheet, include a place for the student's name and a miniature photocopied picture alphabet to which the student can refer. This resource should already be available to students somewhere in the classroom, but for independent writing time it is handy to have it close for near-point copying.

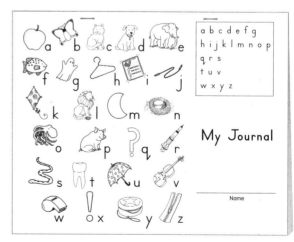

Independent writing journals should have a cover that serves as a reference for letter sounds and letter formation. (See the reproducible form on page 62.)

There are several reasons these simple journals work so well. First, the limited number of pages allows students to fill in the journal over the course of a week or two, and then take it home. In this way, parents continue to see their child's work on a regular basis. Next, students are accustomed to unlined paper at this point and the familiar paper helps them adjust to a journal format. Last, it will cost next to nothing to supply students with these journals.

Of course, the availability of materials in your building and/or preferences that match your teaching style and experience will affect the type of journal you choose. It is important to know why you are incorporating specific aspects in the journals you provide to students and to continually reflect upon how a journal's characteristics may be influencing your student's progress in writing.

Type of Paper

The journal style and format you choose to provide for students at this point may not be as effective a few months down the road as the students' skills and style of writing change over time. One alteration you will make, usually in November, is to fill the journals with lined paper. Kindergartners can go the entire year using unlined paper, but there are several advantages to incorporating lined paper, at some point in the year, for journal writing time.

Paper that has only solid lines approximately ⅝ of an inch apart can assist students in the visual organization and presentation of their writing without forcing them to focus prematurely on placing letters correctly within a dotted-middle-line format. Lined paper signals to students to start their writing at the top of the paper and to move across the paper. Lined paper that is completely filled with lines, except for a small area at the bottom of the page intended for a drawing, will also help students keep their drawings small so they have more space in which to write words. And the boundaries set by the lines can serve as a means for reducing extra-large handwriting. The best advantage of lined paper, however, is that all those lines implicitly encourage students to write more than they might otherwise. I find that if the lines are there, students try to fill them up. Reproducible lined journal pages are provided on pages 63–64.

Be wary of making a blanket change to lined paper for all students; often it works best to move students into lined paper on an individual basis as the need presents itself. Whatever you do, do not use commercially prepared writing paper that has drawing room at the top and a few lines for writing at the bottom. Nothing restricts a student's writing output more than a very limited space in which to write.

Number of Pages

There is a specific reason to assemble the journals with eight to twelve sheets of plain white paper, rather than putting an exact number, such as ten, in each of the journals. As students write daily in their journals and fill them up, you will need to periodically supply students with new journals. This task can be quite time consuming if the entire class needs new journals on the same day. If the first set of journals provided to students do not all have the same number of pages in them (for example, eight to twelve pages instead of a uniform ten for everyone), then students will use them up and need new ones on different days instead of all at the same time. If only a few students need new journals each day, you can incorporate the task into journal writing time, eliminating the need to use precious planning time to prepare new journals.

Whichever approach you use, do not be tempted to construct thicker journals with more than twelve pieces of paper. While it may save a little time, it will interfere with the process of sending home student journals on a regular basis and the students' opportunity to share frequently and to celebrate their writing with their families.

Journal Cover

The cover page that is attached to each journal serves as an important resource during independent writing time. You can create your own, following these pointers, or reproduce the model provided. Ideally, the picture alphabet chosen for the cover page should be an exact replica of the picture alphabet that you have used with the class to chant the letter names and sounds so it will be familiar and accessible to students when they are expected to use it on their own. If you cannot find or create a smaller version of the picture alphabet you have been using with your students, choose another one that has pictures that the students can recognize and name. Keep in mind that the pictures for the vowels should represent the short vowel sounds. If you decide to use a new picture alphabet, take time prior to the first day of independent writing to name all the pictures for the students and review the process for using the pictures to match letters to sounds.

Another useful tool on the cover sheet is a small alphabet of lowercase letters, placed close together. This alphabet should have breaks in the same place as the breaks in the alphabet song (*a, b, c, d, e, f, g / h, i, j, k, l, m, n, o, p / q, r, s / t, u, v / w, x, y, z*) and works well if students need to sing the alphabet to find a specific letter to copy. Students can point to and touch each letter as they sing the song, stopping at the letter for which they are looking. Remember, students will need plenty of opportunities to practice this skill during the first six weeks of guided instruction if you expect them to try it during independent writing time.

NUMBERING JOURNALS

As students get a new journal, I put a number in the bottom right corner to indicate which number journal this is for them (their first, second, third, and so on). I do this for three reasons:

1. It is easier for parents to organize these keepsakes chronologically and see their child's writing development.

2. Students love keeping track of and comparing how many journals they've filled.

3. It provides an opportunity for me to give reminders, such as, "I bet this seventh journal is going to have some periods in it."

My Journal

Name _____

a b c d e f g
h i j k l m n o p
q r s
t u v
w x y z

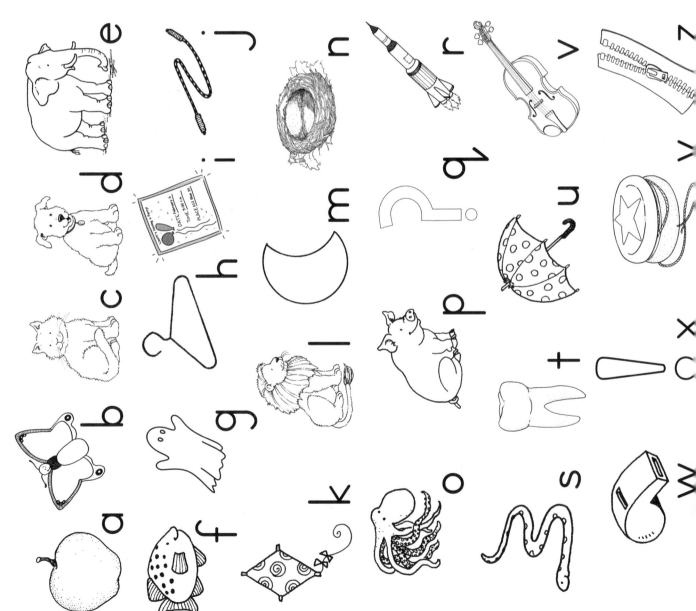

e
d
c
b
a

j
i
h
g
f

n
m
l
k

r
q
p
o

v
u
t
s

z
y
x
w

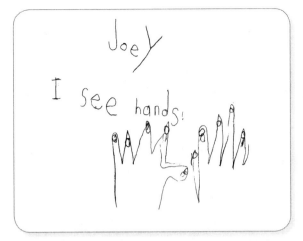

Joey, age 6 Plain, unlined paper works best for guided daily writing at the beginning of the year and for the first several weeks of independent journal writing.

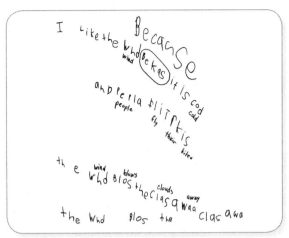

Ricco, age 6 This student is ready to transition to lined paper, which will assist in the organization and presentation of his writing. This structural support will also make it easier for him to read back his writing. The adult handwriting, as seen on this writing sample and most others, is called underwriting. Underwriting is discussed on page 84.

Cami, age 5 This student is practically asking for lined paper and should be provided with it as soon as possible.

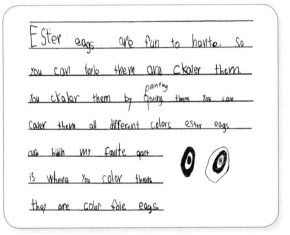

Jayme, age 5 Not only does lined paper assist students in writing more neatly, but it also tends to indirectly encourage students to write more as they feel compelled to fill up the lines. A small, unlined area is available for drawing. This paper works nicely November through May for most students.

WHEN WILL I GET A JOURNAL WITH LINES?

As you start to replace some students' filled journals with journals that have lined paper, most of the other students will begin to inquire as to when they will get lined paper. Telling them that they need lines when they start to write more than one idea will indirectly encourage them to write more.

GROUPING STUDENTS

The progress that students make during the next few months is dependent upon your ability to circulate among students and provide individualized mini-lessons while they are writing in their journals. The process for delivering individualized mini-lessons will be thoroughly explained later in this chapter, but the goal is to circulate and speak to each student three times during each 25- to 30-minute writing session. This is best accomplished with 22 or fewer students. Do not despair, however, if you have more than 22 in your class. Almost every year that I was developing this approach, there were at least 24 students in both the morning and afternoon sessions of my kindergarten classroom. So how did a program that works best for 22 or fewer students get developed and implemented in a classroom with a significantly higher number of students? Some of the students were sent away! Not for good, just during journal-writing time. Here is how it can be done.

If your class size is larger than 22 students, divide the class into four equal heterogeneous groups. For example, a class with 28 students would be divided into four groups of seven students, with approximately the same number of boys and girls who represent a range of motivation and achievement levels. Each group is then rotated out of journal writing time every fourth day. If one of the groups is not participating in journal writing each day, that leaves 21 students writing in their journals. And that means you have time to circulate and conduct individualized mini-lessons effectively (see pages 78–86 for the full lesson cycle).

That solves that, except for what to do with the one-quarter of your class that is not assigned to write. Since the block of time you are dealing with is 25 to 30 minutes long, it does not work particularly well to have these students work on something quietly in the corner while you teach writing to the rest of the class. The time period is usually too long. If at all possible, arrange for another adult to assist you in the classroom during this time to supervise an activity with the small group of remaining students.

KEEPING TRACK OF STUDENT GROUPS AND MATERIALS

An easy way to identify the four student groups you have created for a rotating schedule is to assign a color to each group. When you or your students write their names on their journals, use a marker that corresponds with the color group to which you have assigned them. For example, you may have six students with their names written in green, seven students with their names written in orange, seven in the red group, and six in the purple group. Make a list for yourself and for the other adults who are coming into your classroom during writing time that shows which students are in what group. Also, make a note of the rotation schedule so all adults will know which students are not writing on any particular day.

This list of student groups is arranged in a sequence that serves as a mnemonic device (GORP: green, orange, red, purple). It helps adults in the room remember the rotation order.

Green	Orange	Red	Purple
Camille	Madison	Addy	Amelia
Joe	Alec	Justin	Dean
Isabela	Toni	Tally	Christina
Thomas	Joey	Ricco	Caleb
Frances	Yasmin	Mackenzie	Taylor
Gena	Jacob	Ruby	Dane
	Anthony	Jayme	

Options for Assistance

■ Instructional Aides

Though instructional aides usually arrive at work at the same time students start school, they are often under-used at this time. Instructional aides may therefore be available for the first half-hour to work in your classroom. Another idea is to offer to trade some of the aide time that may be scheduled for your classroom later in the day for aide time during writing.

■ Speech and language specialist

Because daily writing incorporates so many language skills and because students with speech and language needs can often be supported through this approach, the speech and language specialist in your building might be willing to schedule his or her in-class service during your writing time. The first half-hour of the day can be a difficult period to pull students from classrooms, and the speech and language specialist just might be free at that time.

■ Special Education Teacher

Just as the speech and language specialist might like the idea of delivering services during your writing time, so might the special education teacher. Often specialists will agree to share the load; that is, they may feel that working with the small group of students who are rotated out of writing for the day—even if none of their students with disabilities are in the group—is a worthwhile tradeoff if it means you, the classroom teacher, are better able to meet the written-language and fine-motor needs of students with disabilities whom they also support. This type of collaboration, where all professionals share service delivery to provide more frequent and relevant services, works well to address scheduling demands in schools.

■ Title I Teacher

If any of your students receive Title I services, speak to the Title I teacher about the possibility of addressing those students' needs in the classroom with a co-teaching model that can benefit all students. Consider the early reading skills you can teach together through daily writing: letter names, letter sounds, letter-sound correspondence, directionality, sight words, main idea, and reading when it comes time to review what has been written each day. Once specialists understand how you will be teaching writing, they may be even more agreeable to working with you in the classroom during your writing time instead of coming in later in the day or pulling students from the classroom all together.

■ Parent Volunteers

Parents of kindergartners are often interested in being involved with their child's school experience since it is a fresh beginning and may be the first time they are entrusting their children to other adults. Make the most of this. Let parents know right away at the beginning of the school year that you would love to have them in the classroom and are going to be in need of parent volunteers beginning in October. At the beginning of September, send home a friendly note in clear language that explains why you need parent volunteers during writing time, what their responsibilities will be, and which days you need help. The note can also outline the benefits of volunteering in the classroom. Include a tear-off portion at the bottom of the note where a parent can include his or her name, phone number, and preferred day(s). If your writing time is the first event of the morning, emphasize to parents the convenience of volunteering in the classroom before work or tending to other responsibilities, when they are already at school dropping their child off for the day. A sample letter is included at right.

■ Grandparents

By September, you may have noticed that some of your students have grandparents who are actively involved in their lives, perhaps even as the primary caregivers who are responsible for raising the children. If this is the case, be inclusive in your note and be sure it welcomes grandparents in as volunteers. Also consider unofficial grandparents—seniors who are active in the school, an elderly person you know who could benefit from getting out more often, or the wealth of resources available through a partnership with a community group composed of members who are retired yet active in their community.

■ Rotating School Personnel

Having tapped the resources mentioned above, there may be one or two days a week when you still need an extra pair of hands in the classroom to work with the group of students who are not writing on those days. There are other personnel in the building who, although they probably could not commit to assisting every day, might be willing to fill in one or more of your holes each week. Speak with your principal, librarian, counselor, or anyone else who might be interested in donating a half-hour of his or her time. Your principal may be the best choice, in that he or she needs to know what is going on in classrooms, and may be even more intrigued because you are trying a new approach to teaching writing with your kindergartners.

If all else fails, you may have one or two days a week when the small group of students will be held responsible for themselves and will need to be involved in an activity without the help of an adult. Because the groups rotate out of writing every fourth day, a different group each week would need to take this time.

Some suggestions for activities that require supervision and others intended for independent work follow on page 70.

WOULDN'T IT BE SIMPLER AND MORE EFFECTIVE TO HAVE ALL STUDENTS WRITE IN THEIR JOURNALS EVERY DAY?

If you are wondering about the effect of having students miss instructional time in writing every fourth day, rest assured that this approach was developed with large classes—and that the solution of rotating groups was the only one that allowed me to implement daily writing instruction successfully. By doing this, you are not shortchanging your students; you are managing your classroom in a way that allows you to provide more intensely individualized instruction on a regular basis as well as avoid the predicament of students practicing writing without proper guidance, feedback, and closure. Allowing such a situation to repeatedly occur will eventually result in lower writing achievement for students.

Dear Parents,

As you know, your kindergartners have been participating in daily drawing and writing lessons during the first half-hour of class each day. I demonstrate and talk about the thinking and skills beginning readers and writers need, and the students learn by copying my model. Soon, they will have enough knowledge to begin writing on their own.

Independent journal writing, where our students draw and write on their own while I circulate about the room and assist them, will start in October. This new format will allow me to teach students on a more individual basis. However, since our class is fairly large, I could greatly use some assistance during this time. I am looking for parent or grandparent volunteers to supervise a small group of students who will not be writing on any given day. The small group would be participating in one of the following activities—all of which require absolutely no experience on your part—and I will always be close by to assist as needed:

- checking out a book from our classroom library
- working on the computer
- sharing their journal writing
- illustrating or sharing books they have written
- practicing reading and writing sight words
- doing a free-choice activity

Volunteering in the classroom has many benefits. You will get to know the students in the class, gain a better understanding of the classroom expectations and routines, and experience the joy of being involved in and observing the development of our students' reading and writing skills. Most important, you get to watch your young learner in action.

Our writing time is scheduled from _____ to _____. Please indicate below which day(s) of the week would be most convenient for you. Thank you so much!

Sincerely,

[tear-off section of letter]

I am interested in volunteering in the classroom during writing time beginning in October. The following day(s) work best for me:

____ Monday   ____ Tuesday   ____ Wednesday   ____ Thursday   ____ Friday

Name _____   Phone #s _____

Activities With Supervision

If you have instructional aides or parent or community volunteers coming in to work with the group that is not scheduled to write, then you will be solely in charge of determining what will be happening with these students. Think of this not as just another block of time for which something needs to be planned; instead, consider this the opportunity to do something you have always wanted to do with your kindergarten students but just did not have the time or manpower to do. Activities that require no training on the part of the adult and do not necessarily need the consistency of the same adult from day to day will work best. Ideas for this group include:

- journal sharing
- computer time
- reading time
- small-group read-aloud
- checking out a book to take home
- reviewing and working with words on the word wall
- doing an art project
- any number of activities from which kindergarten students can benefit, especially when it would be valuable if the interaction occurred in a small group

Activities Without Supervision

If you absolutely cannot find any adults to work in your classroom during this time, you have two choices. The first is to have all of your students writing, but to put the group that is not scheduled to write at designated tables where they will not receive individualized mini-lessons that day. They will not be excluded; you will just have to make a conscious effort to spend more time with the other three-fourths of your class.

The second option is to brainstorm activities that the small group of students who are not writing could do on their own. These activities would have to be quiet, engage all students in the group, reinforce important skills, and not require assistance from you. Such activities might include literacy skill-building computer games (provided you have enough computers in your room) or independent center activities. This may be a way to squeeze in some free-choice time. Remember, this is six weeks into the school year, when students have had plenty of time to learn what your expectations are for working quietly and not disrupting the teaching or learning that is going on in the classroom.

WHAT IF I AM BLESSED WITH A SMALL CLASS AND A FULL-TIME AIDE?

If you have a full-time aide and do not need him or her to supervise students during writing time, have the aide pull students aside, one at a time, for about five minutes and work on each student's current area of need. Ideas include working on letter names and sounds, reading and writing sight words, and letter formation. Not only will students get some individual attention and instruction a few times per week, they'll also get in 20 minutes of writing, even on the days they work with the aide.

REVISITING ROOM ARRANGEMENT

Since you will not be providing direct whole-group instruction during independent writing, you do not need to take overhead visibility into consideration and you may rearrange the configuration of student desks if you like. On the other hand, you may have discovered that using the overhead is very effective and therefore want to maintain this seating arrangement for teaching at other times during the day. Do try to maintain an arrangement that enables students to see the classroom word wall from where they will be sitting while they write. If this is not possible, remind students that they may move about the room during writing time to read the word wall, word lists, and other resources around the room. (Of course, this reminder applies to all students, regardless of seating arrangement.)

Each day before writing time, lay out the journals at the tables or areas that are used for writing. Your placement of the journals will signal to students where they are supposed to sit. Since there is no permanent seating arrangement, students benefit from sitting in a variety of places and working near different students each day. For this reason, be deliberate about mixing up the journals each time you lay them out. You will naturally take into consideration:

- where to seat students to maximize learning and minimize off-task behaviors

- how to group students to encourage peer learning

- how to strategically place students who need the most support (I recommend seating these students at a table end or near an empty chair so when you find yourself lingering at their spots to help them you can more easily have a seat and stay for a while.)

If the class is large and you have decided to have just three-fourths of your students writing each day, you will lay out journals for only the three groups scheduled to write. It is not necessary to draw students' attention to which group they are in. Rather, train them to enter the classroom and look for their names on their journals; if they do not see their journals laying out they should go to the area of the classroom where there is an alternative activity planned.

DAILY JOURNAL WRITING TOPICS

Once the logistics are in place and the journals are prepared, the only planning you need to do during the months of October, November, December, and January is to come up with a topic for students to draw and write about each day in their journals. This might immediately create some cognitive dissonance; isn't the whole idea of journal writing that students write about whatever they want to write about so that it is meaningful to them? Most writing programs, and thus many teachers, have latched onto this idea and applied it to writing in a kindergarten classroom, without first stopping to think about whether it is appropriate for this age group.

To this point, the majority of your kindergarten students have only had one experience with daily writing and that is you standing in front of them walking them through a drawing step by step and assisting them in writing a word, phrase, or sentence to go with the drawing. It is not realistic to suddenly expect them to draw and write about something without providing some guidance, which in this case is an idea for them—an idea that is carefully chosen and will lead to their having a successful writing experience. Providing a topic gets students excited and gets them going, especially if, for the first few days of journal writing, the topic is something they have drawn and written about prior to this with the class. Yes, topics must be meaningful, and for daily journal writing to work, it is up to you to choose meaningful topics with which the students can be successful.

Selecting Effective Topics

As you ponder topics for the first few days of independent writing, choose topics your students can draw easily and then readily formulate an idea about. Since drawing still comes first, it is their ability to draw the topic that will be the deciding factor in whether they can get started working independently. For the first few days, select a topic that you have used during the previous six weeks of whole-group instruction. Students will recall enough about how to draw the picture as well as what they might write about it. My students are always thrilled the first day of independent journal writing because they get to draw the Busy Bee all by themselves and, since it is such a vital part of our classroom, they all have something to say about it. (See Joe's first independent journal entry on page 21.) Also, try to choose a topic that will allow students to use some of the words they already know but will also require them to try new words.

As the weeks and months pass and students become more and more productive and successful with writing in their journals, you can get more creative and less calculating with the writing topics you assign. After the first week or two of independent journal writing, when students realize they have the skills to draw and write a little independently, a broader range of topics will serve them better. The best source for topic ideas is the content you use throughout the rest of the day. Characters from read-alouds or shared reading books, upcoming holidays that are part of the curriculum, words from word families that are being studied, field trips, the weather, or any other high-interest science or social studies topics are all effective subject matter for writing time. Your curriculum and calendar will generate a unique list of topics, as shown by the sample topic list from my own lessons, below.

Sample Topics for Independent Journal Writing

Topic	Why It Was Chosen
Busy Bee	class mascot; introduce independent writing with a very familiar topic
traffic light	safety lesson; practice color words; practice drawing basic shapes
bus	field trip (students had just taken a class trip on a school bus)
apples	unit of study; practice color words
leaves	fall season theme; practice color words
cat	favorite topic; practice the -at chunk
a time to call 911	unit of study; assess understanding
Little Red Hen	shared reading; check comprehension of the story
flag	Pledge of Allegiance; reinforce the pledge
dad/mom	favorite topics; practice writing these high-frequency words
The Giving Tree	read aloud; practice the -ing chunk
Frosty the Snowman	winter/snow theme
100th Day of School	math event
number story	math topic; practice formulating and writing short stories that involve combining numbers or taking away a number
Abraham Lincoln	social studies unit of study
weather	science unit of study
class picture	class activity
Dr. Seuss	celebration of Dr. Seuss's birthday

Keeping a record of the topics you assign and taking notes on their overall effectiveness will assist you in selecting topics the following year. Trial and error will show which topics are most successful, as indicated by the smiles on students' faces, their enthusiasm, and the amount and quality of writing the topics elicit.

The writing samples included below on the next two pages, although not all from October, November, December, and January, show how carefully selecting a topic can help students write more fluently and generate an incredible amount of enthusiasm and pride in their work.

Benefits of Providing Topics

Many teachers who try free-choice journal writing with their kindergartners become discouraged when they discover that their students tend to write about the same thing over and over again and consequently do not take any risks with new drawings or new words. Not only does a teacher-selected topic encourage students to write about a variety of subjects, it provides a strong focus. Students feel compelled to write about the assigned topic and nothing else. In the long run, students learn to contemplate a topic and stay on topic while writing, rather than jumping from one topic to another, a habit that many young writers develop when they write without enough support and guidance. And, if you provide an engaging topic, there is no writing time wasted while students sit and think about something in which they might be interested in writing.

Carefully chosen topics can serve as a review or a way to reinforce something that was previously taught in the classroom. It is possible to ascertain in just a sentence or two if a child comprehended an important point in a lesson, as evidenced in Caleb's writing about the moon on page 75.

Often, ideas or characters from books used for shared reading or read aloud are made into journal writing topics and what amazing results this yields! Some students rewrite entire stories (a retell in written format, requiring fluent and advanced writing skills) while others choose to summarize (an extremely advanced thinking skill for kindergartners). (See Thomas's summary on page 75.) Students may even write their own versions of stories they have heard.

As the weeks and months go on, some students may inform you that they want to write about something other than the given topic. This marks an important transition and indicates that they have discovered that writing is an outlet for something they currently feel the need to express. By all means, when students start to ask if they can write about something other than the assigned topic, please say yes!

Toni, age 5 This journal entry followed a discussion of individuals with visual impairments.

Tally, age 5 This student found a creative way to write about the weather.

Hikre Dike Dock the maos
Wit up the klok the
klok Strak onel the
maws ran Down
Hikre Dike Dock
the maws is fun
I like the maws

Christina, age 5 The topic *Hickory, Dickory Dock* led to this student writing more than she probably would have otherwise. Note she added two more sentences because she finished writing the nursery rhyme before writing time was over but knew she was expected to continue writing.

Deanna, age 6 The student's writing reflects her comprehension of a read-aloud book about bats.

I like being quiet
I have a quiet club my quiet
club has quiet toys. The quiet
toys do not make a sand if
they do I thqhou them
out! uut you go!

Lee, age 5 The word *quiet* was chosen for the topic so students could practice lowercase *q* and its sound in context.

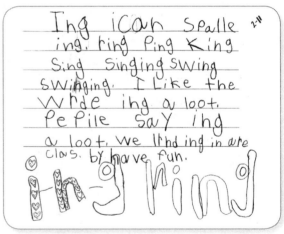

Claire, age 5 The chunk *ing* had just been introduced to the students. Having them write about it on several different days helped them realize what they knew about it and that they were capable of using it in their writing.

One day there was two 4-6
rabits playing thin three mror
rabits thin four mror and that
moks 2+3+4=9. One day there
was five brass they ron
thin five baby
brass came and
ron t and that
mayke 5+5=10

Frances, age 6 The topic *number story* let this student demonstrate her understanding of both writing and math concepts.

You can see
the moon at
nit and You can
see the moon
at morning and
it lax looks (like) ise its
gloweg but ise its
not gloingo
the san sun is (liting)
it (up)

Caleb, age 5 *The moon*, a topic that we had studied in science, presented the perfect opportunity for this student to demonstrate his understanding of a complex concept.

What dose your house
look like? How olde are
you? what coler shert
aer you waering? How
was your Easter?

Mackenzie, age 5 The topic *questions for the principal* encouraged students to formulate questions, find and copy the *wh-* question words, and practice putting question marks at the ends of their questions.

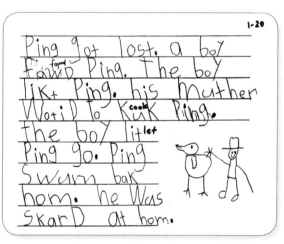

Ping got lost. a boy 1-20
fawid found Ping. The boy
likt Ping. his muther
votid to kuk cook Ping.
the boy litlet let
Ping go. Ping
swum bak
hom. he was
skard at hom.

Thomas, age 5 The chunk *ing* had just been introduced to the students. Having the students write about it on several different days helped them use it in context—in this case, retelling a story.

FACILITATING INDEPENDENT WRITING TIME

Before the first day of independent writing in October, begin getting your students accustomed to the idea of writing on their own. You can do this by regularly commenting on their developing skills during whole-group lessons. For example, you might say, "Wow! You're getting so good at listening to sounds and writing down the right letters—I know you are ready to start writing by yourselves!" The point is to build up their confidence and help them, as is always necessary with kindergartners, to become cognizant of what they know and what they are capable of doing. You'll also want to prepare them for a new format. As independent writing time approaches, let your students know that the time is coming soon when you will no longer stand in front of them and help them with every step of their writing.

As I recommended in Chapter 2, be sure you have modeled and discussed these key procedures and skills repeatedly, prior to beginning independent writing. This preparation work will make the transition away from whole-group, guided lessons less overwhelming.

- Know and think about the topic that has been given for the day.
- Draw a picture first. Put the drawing at the bottom of the paper.
- Draw as well as you can and do not worry if the picture on your paper does not match exactly the picture you have in your mind.
- Add details to help others understand what you are trying to draw.
- Do not spend too much time drawing; you will need time to write letters and words.
- Think of some words to write that go with the picture.
- Count how many words you are going to write.
- Think about the first word; determine if it is a word you already know or if it is a word for which you are going to try and listen to the sounds.
- Write the word, or write the letters for as many of the sounds as you can hear.
- If you know a place in the classroom where you can find out how to write the entire word or one of the letters that makes a sound you hear, take the time to find it and copy it, even if you have to get out of your chair.
- If you are not sure about a word or a sound, try your hardest and then move on.
- When you finish the first word, use a finger space to show that you are starting a new word.
- Write the rest of the words in your sentence, using as many sounds and letters as you know and putting a finger space in between the words.
- When you are all done, put a period at the end of your sentence.
- Touch each word you write with your finger and read it to see if it sounds right to you.
- If writing time is not yet over, add some additional details to your picture or write some more words to go with your picture.

You surely do not need to emphasize all of these things during each lesson. This list is just a reminder of the task analysis that students will need to be familiar with in order to draw a picture and write a sentence about it. Your talking about and modeling each step over and over again during the first six weeks of school will give students the background knowledge they need and the guided practice necessary to assist them in trying it on their own.

Getting Started

Soon, you will not need to address the class as a whole, other than to inform them of the writing topic for the day. However, you will need to briefly lead the session for the first several days in October. As students enter the classroom (or begin the writing period) the first day that they will be using their journals, get them excited by making an announcement that today is the day they get to try writing all by themselves in their brand-new journals. Each student should look for the journal that has his or her name on it. Since you will be doing some explaining the first day, put out all the journals and keep all students together for your instruction (do not yet send one group to do an alternative activity, if you will be rotating groups for independent writing). After a day or two, when students understand the basics about procedures and expectations, you can start working with just three-quarters of the students each day.

Once students are all seated in front of their journals on the first day, say something along these lines: "Remember how I've been telling you that you're going to start writing in your journals all by yourselves? Well, this is the first day you get to give it a try. This kind of journal has your name on the front and that means you don't have to write your name on your paper every day. We already know it belongs to you." Have students point to their names. "Let's look at the front of our journals. Do you see the alphabet with the pictures? Remember when we used the pictures in the alphabet book to find out which letters we needed to write on our papers? Now you have your very own set of pictures and you get to try and use the pictures all by yourself." Pause and give students a few seconds to look at the pictures. (They will probably check to see if these are the same pictures that are in the picture alphabet you have been using during writing time.) "Okay, let's open our journals to the first clean white page."

Make sure each student starts on the first page and, in days to follow, learns how to turn to the very next sheet of available paper in his or her journal. This will result in a more sequential record of the students' writing. Also, show students how to fold the cover of their journals completely back and underneath the other sheets. Not doing so will result in crowded tables with overlapping journals and squabbling students. Help students with this as needed, until it becomes a standard routine.

Announcing the Topic

Coach students with the process of getting started, beginning with a familiar writing topic on the first few days. "Today we are going to write about the Busy Bee [or whatever topic you have chosen]. What do you think we should do first in our journals—draw a picture of the Busy Bee or write some words about the Busy Bee?" Students will surely know to draw the picture first. "And are we going to draw the picture at the top of the paper or the bottom of the paper?" Remind them to put the picture toward the bottom and to start writing their words at the top of the paper so they have plenty of room to include all the words they want. "Okay, start drawing. You know how to do it."

Circulate around the room and encourage any students who feel anxious because you are not walking them through it step-by-step. When a few students are nearing the end of their drawings, have the entire class stop and look at you while you give the next directions. "Soon it is going to be time to start writing some words about the Busy Bee. We've done this before, and I know you know what to do. Just in case, here are some ideas. You can put the letter *b* because we can hear it, you can spell the whole word out if you want to, or you can write a whole sentence about your picture, like *I can see the bee* or *The bee is flying*. I love the pictures you're drawing, and I can't wait to see the letters you write on your papers."

Over the next few days you will speak less and less to the group as a whole and more to students on an individual basis. The students are transitioning into writing independently while you are moving more toward working with individual students and their specific needs rather than trying to address the needs of the group as a whole. Within a very short time, all you will need to say to the group is, "We're writing about _____ today." Because students seem to come in and get settled at different speeds during the first five minutes or so, you might end up restating the topic to individuals or small groups of students as they come to their seats at various times. However, do keep your expectations high—that all students be seated and working quietly on their drawings within two or three minutes of entering the classroom.

You may often need to repeat the rule of first drawing about the topic and then writing about it. Drawing before attempting to write will make most students feel that they can get started on their own, even if they have limited letter-sound correspondence skills. Like most rules, however, it will not be hard and fast. If students are capable and excited to begin with writing rather than drawing, allow and encourage this; they can surely draw after putting their ideas down in writing, or maybe not even draw at all.

Reinforcing Behavior Conducive to Learning

If you took the time and energy to establish high behavior expectations during the first six weeks of school, then you will have an easy job ahead of you as you move into independent journal writing time. Students will already know that they are expected to be engaged in the activity. And they will assume the expectation to work up to their potential is still in place. However, with a little less instructional guidance from you, some students may revert to disruptive behaviors or not work up to their potential. Your scaffolding and steadfast expectation that they work up to their potential each day will help re-establish positive learning behaviors.

Once students realize they can draw and write without you walking them through everything step-by-step, and that writing independently is rewarding, their overall willingness and yearning to write will intensify. Writing time will soon become the time of day when students are most likely to behave and participate to their fullest. This is true even of students who have difficulty writing and do not show improvement as quickly and easily as the other students. Students will typically not act out during writing because they will experience success as they work at their own levels and their own rates of progress.

TEACHING INDIVIDUALIZED MINI-LESSONS

At the heart of this writing approach is teaching targeted, timely, individualized mini-lessons during independent journal writing. Individualized mini-lessons will make it possible for you to scaffold your instruction for each student, allowing all students to progress steadily with no ceiling on their learning.

You may be familiar with the idea of a group mini-lesson, which is usually taught to the whole class on a daily basis prior to students participating in an activity in which they are encouraged to try out or apply the skills addressed in the mini-lesson. For example, in a traditional writers' workshop approach to teaching writing, the teacher might start the writing session with his or her entire class gathered around for a mini-lesson about spacing between words. The teacher would probably show some writing that has spaces between words, compare it to writing without spaces, and demonstrate how putting spaces between the words we write makes our writing easier to read. The students would then be sent to write, with a reminder that today they should definitely try to use spaces in their journals.

The problem that arises with whole-group mini-lessons is that the particular skill being taught on any given day may only be appropriate, in a scaffolded instruction sense, for about one-third of the class. If a typical group of 21 students, all of whom have been through the six weeks of whole-group instruction on drawing and labeling pictures, listened to a review lesson on spacing, most likely one-third of them would already understand the purpose of spacing between words and have been applying this skill on a regular basis in their daily writing. Another one-third of the students would not yet be capable of understanding or using the skill being taught because this group is able to write only one or two letters for one-word labels during journal writing (in fact, some students may not yet understand the concept of a word). Only the last one-third of the class may be at a point in their development where they can truly benefit from a lesson on spacing between words. Because whole-group mini-lessons are rarely timely and appropriate for all of the students in any given class, your instruction will instead consist of brief, timely, highly personalized mini-lessons.

How is this possible? Teachers frequently say, "If only I had more time to work with my students one-on-one . . ." The key to implementing individualized mini-lessons is not to find more time. The solution is to adjust the notion of what exactly a mini-lesson is: a targeted, very brief nugget of instruction.

When you walk past a student's seat and remind him or her to start writing at the top of the paper, with one brief comment that does not even require you to slow down, this is a mini-lesson for that student. This lesson format takes less than five seconds, requires no special materials or forethought, wastes not a second of the other students' time, and is a very meaningful lesson for that child at that particular moment. While not all individualized mini-lessons will be one sentence long and require less than five seconds of your time, you must stay focused and keep them very brief. The trade-off for not going in depth is having the opportunity to address each student's specific, immediate, and dynamic needs and to repeat the lessons as needed.

In whole-group lessons, students often do benefit from hearing a teacher talk about something they have already mastered and are applying in writing on a regular basis. To them, the lesson may be a review, but it helps solidify an understanding in their minds about how or when the skill should be used. It also serves the purpose of allowing students to assess whether they fully understand the skills and have been using them correctly in their writing. Likewise, students profit when they hear instruction for which they are not quite academically ready.

The same thing happens when you give individualized mini-lessons. Students will naturally stop and listen to the mini-lessons that are directed at students who are seated near them. They will momentarily focus their attention on that student's writing, what you are saying about it, and make a comparison between it and their own writing. In this way, they will reap the benefits of receiving a quick review, a confirmation that they are doing things correctly, or a preview of what you might soon be expecting from them. It is not necessary to ask students to listen to another student's mini-lesson or insist that they do; just always indicate that it is acceptable and advantageous to do so. This strategy will also save time for you. When you observe a student other than the intended recipient of the mini-lesson listening and comprehending what you are saying, and if that mini-lesson includes a timely and appropriate teaching point for the student who was listening in, you may say something along the lines of, "And the same for you. I would be able to read your writing better if you would put just a few more sounds in your words." You will not necessarily need to model again how to include another sound if that student has just watched you do it.

To make this approach even more effective, be sure to mix up the seating arrangement each day so that students are able to observe the writing and hear the individualized mini-lessons given to all of their classmates.

Conferring

A common feature of writers' workshop and similar writing programs is the practice of conferring with students. Conferring allows students time to talk about their writing. It also provides teachers time to assess where students are with their skills as well as give feedback or direct one-on-one instruction. In a typical writers' workshop, teachers can make time to confer with students once or twice a week, depending on the way they structure and manage their writing time. Conferring often happens at a table in a quiet corner of the room so the teacher and student can talk without being interrupted. Meanwhile, the other students in the class continue to write and write and write, possibly repeating mistakes that will develop into poor writing habits; or, students sit and sit and sit, helpless because they cannot find a way to go on without the assistance of the teacher, who is tied up in individual student conferences. As it turns out, students who are not currently having a conference with the teacher are not receiving instruction or getting regular feedback, two requirements for supporting their growth in writing.

For writing instruction to be successful in a kindergarten classroom, you must find a way to check in with students at least once, and hopefully more than once, each writing session. This can be accomplished by circulating throughout the period rather than being grounded at a table. It is not necessary to eliminate the whole idea of conferring; it is, however, imperative to learn how to do it quickly and on-the-move in order to reach all students each day during a standard 25- to 30-minute period of writing.

The GLOW, GROW, SO Formula

There are no rules about what should and should not be accomplished during an individualized mini-lesson. The only guideline is to address the current instructional needs of each student and take advantage of the best possible teaching point as you pass by each student's seat. It is highly effective to combine Vygotsky's (1978) idea of a zone of proximal development with Bruner and Sherwood's (1975) concept of scaffolding. Simply put, recognize what a child is capable of doing and build upon that knowledge to teach new skills and expect a little bit more each day.

For most individualized mini-lessons, a basic three-part formula works nicely to move students from trying a new skill to the point of demonstrating that skill or concept on a consistent basis. The first two parts of this formula may be familiar to you as you have probably used them often in your teaching and in other aspects of your life.

- GLOW: First, find something positive in the student's drawing or writing, something that definitely meets the criteria of following the directions or doing it the way you suggested. For example, if the topic for the day was *brown bear,* and the student drew a bear and then copied the word *brown* from the color chart posted in the classroom, your comment might be, "I'm impressed that you remembered where to find the word *brown* in our classroom."

- GROW: Immediately following that, address the most pertinent teaching point, something that will allow you to scaffold your instruction to the next level. In this case, you might say, "What about the word *bear*? Is that a word we learned? Is it on the word wall?" (The student should say no, since it is not a high-frequency word, but if not, you can remind him or her that *bear* is not a word the class has learned.) "Then you'll need to listen closely to the sounds in *bear* and write down some of the sounds you hear."

These two parts of the formula together are called GLOW and GROW, where you point out something the student has done well—something that makes his or her writing glow—and then suggest something upon which the student can improve, something that will help the student grow. What makes this approach so effective is the third and final part of the formula, a part that is possible only because you are up and moving and checking students' writing two or three times during each writing session.

- SO: Tell the student what you expect to see when you circulate around the next time. You might say, "So, when I come back around I want to see some sounds on your paper for the word *bear*." This expectation to immediately apply the skill or instruction, coupled with you actually checking back and providing some final feedback, is what keeps students steadily moving along the continuum of learning.

It is quite natural to teach with this three-part formula, complimenting a student on something he or she did, suggesting a way to improve it, and expecting the student to try to implement the suggestion. (Sample mini-lessons for October–April appear in Chapter 6.)

Circulating the First Time (First Individualized Mini-lesson)

Once all the students are settled and working, begin your first trip around the room for your first set of individualized mini-lessons. If students raise their hands because they need you, or get out of their seats and come to you, try to ascertain exactly what each student needs. If it is their writing with which students need help, gently remind them that they may not get out of their seats and come to you during journal writing time and that you will come to them instead. This general expectation will allow you to continue moving about the room and ensure that all students routinely get an equal amount of attention and instruction.

The purposes for circulating this first time around the room are:

- Quickly greet each and every student.

- Record the date on each student's paper. (The students may copy the date onto their papers later in the school year, but for now the focus needs to be on drawing and writing.)

- Ensure that everyone has started on his or her writing.

- Provide encouragement or ideas on how to begin for those who have not yet done so.

Start circulating as soon as possible and go directly to any student who is already seated and writing. Though the term *circulate* implies you will be moving in a circular or systematic fashion about the room, in actuality you will jump from the most timely teaching situation to the next, all the while mindful that you are getting to each student an equal number of times. The first time you circulate around the room should take approximately ten minutes. In a class of 20 students, that allows you about 30 seconds per student. Some students will need just five seconds from you this time around the room, while others may need two or three minutes. Briefly greet each student with either a comment about something from the day before ("Did you lose that tooth yet?") or a general hello ("How are you today? I'm so happy to see you."), jot the date in the corner of the page, and then address the writing at hand. By personally greeting each student before discussing writing, the students will recognize that you are interested in them and happy to see them. This little touch often gives students the confidence and trust needed to move forward with their writing.

If a student already has something on his paper, comment on the fact that he has started and then mention what you hope to see when you come back around. For example, if the student is busy drawing a picture, you can say, "I like how you got going right away on your picture. The next time I come to talk to you I bet you'll have some words on your paper that I can read." The GLOW and SO parts of the formula are being used first here, and once the student has some writing on his paper the teacher will have some material on which to base a GROW comment. If you encounter a student who has started working but is not following your suggestions—using the given topic, drawing a picture first, putting the picture at the bottom of the paper, or beginning his or her writing at the top of the paper—address the issue right away during your first time around.

Often the lines between the first and subsequent times to circulate about the classroom get blurred. Because quite a few minutes will have passed by the time you get toward the end of your first trip about the room, the last several students you greet may be well into their writing, which may mean that they receive their main individualized mini-lesson for the day rather than just a hello and some encouragement to get started. If a teachable moment presents itself, do not refrain from teaching just because it is your first time around the room.

Circulating the Second Time

The second time around the classroom during writing time is when the most intensive instruction will occur. By the time you have greeted all students and recorded the date in their journals, students should be well enough into their writing that you can readily see a teaching point to address for each of them. Chapter 6 contains many suitable individualized mini-lessons based on actual kindergarten student writing samples, many of which clearly show what the student was independently drawing or writing, the intervention by the teacher via an individualized mini-lesson, and the subsequent writing. Refer to this section for examples on how to provide a quick, personalized mini-lesson for every student every day.

The basic three-part formula for an individualized mini-lesson—GLOW, GROW, SO—will be put to best use during this second time around the room. Sometimes it will be necessary to stay next to a student to help him or her carry out your expectation (the SO part of the formula). When this is the case, the student will get a longer individualized mini-lesson that day (consequently, some of the other students may receive mini-lessons that are shorter than usual). This is perfectly fine for teaching situations that require more modeling and assistance than a few passing comments can afford. Also keep in mind that these extended mini-lessons need to be directed to all students, not just struggling students. To make the best use of your time, begin circulating to other students when the student you're working with is ready to carry out your SO request. Unless the student needs your direct guidance, check back with him or her during your third trip around the room.

Although the GLOW, GROW, SO formula works well in many instances and will require students to attempt more difficult skills than they might otherwise, it is not always appropriate to use. For example, if you observe a student applying what was expected of him or her the day before, without any reminders from you, this may be enough to expect for the day. Or, if a student has nothing on his or her paper and therefore is in no position to receive a typical individualized mini-lesson, the lesson could be on how to get started or on the consequences of choosing not to write anything during writing time. Also, at times it may be faster and just as effective to combine the three parts of the formula into one sentence. "It looks like you've drawn a really good picture with a lot of details, so what do you need to do next?"

Erasing

It will be necessary to establish your policy on erasing right away. Erasing is a skill that kindergartners can master, but they do need to be taught how to do it properly. Students need to know that to erase is to get rid of a mark entirely or as much as is physically possible. Talk about how much time and muscle it takes to erase. Also, point out the fact that erasing can often backfire, making more of a mess than was originally there by leaving a dark smear on the paper. Therefore, it makes sense to teach and encourage students to think first before writing so that fewer changes will need to be made. (It also makes sense to do what you can to ensure students have quality erasers that will result in positive erasing experiences.)

You can set some guidelines for erasing so that students are responsible for their mistakes without wholesale erasing. Encourage them to erase if:

- they wrote the wrong letter
- they formed a letter incorrectly and want to try it again
- they need to add in a space

When students erase large portions of their work, they inadvertently delete their thinking processes and writing attempts, which you need to see in order to better teach them. Erasing is also hard work and time consuming. It is not how students should be spending the majority of their journal writing time.

There will be several instances, while you are circulating about the room and delivering individualized mini-lessons, when students need to write something in another way or write it better than they already have. When asking students to do this, be sure to remind them that they should not erase what they already have on their papers. They should just try it again in an empty space. You might draw a practice box on their papers to help them try again within the boundaries of the box. This helps avoid the often messy processes of erasing and trying again in the same place.

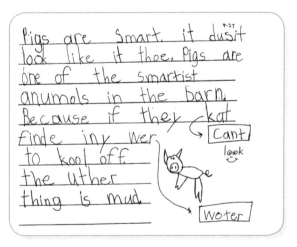

Taylor, age 5 Practice boxes helped Taylor use better sounds for the words *can't* and *water*. When circling back to the student, I needed only to glance at the practice boxes to recall what we had discussed and to determine if she had followed through with it.

Elvis, age 5 With underwriting, this journal entry reveals a charming message and shows that this student is a partially phonetic writer.

Underwriting

Underwriting (Feldgus & Cardonick, 1999) refers to a teacher's act of transcribing in standard form a student's emergent writing. The original intent of underwriting was to model the correct writing of certain words, as well as provide a correctly written model to assist a student in later rereading what he or she had written. When you apply underwriting to daily journal writing, however, its primary intent is to expedite the process of implementing individualized mini-lessons while you circulate about the classroom.

Benefits of Underwriting Much of kindergarten writing cannot yet be read by others, but it is beneficial to be able to look back at a student's writing and know what message he or she was trying to convey. Your consistent use of underwriting will ensure that this is possible. Use underwriting flexibly; find a way that both suits you and maximizes student learning. The following points outline how underwriting can increase the overall effectiveness of your writing instruction.

- During each journal writing period, you may read up to 22 journal entries. Part of the individualized mini-lessons will be to have the students read back what they have written. If this is difficult for a particular student and you cannot offer much assistance because you cannot tell exactly what was written, it makes sense, once the writing is finally deciphered, to jot it down. That way, when you circulate around the room and come upon the same student, you do not need to spend another two or three minutes recalling what it was that he or she wrote.

- You may be asked to describe a student's capabilities in detail. This may be necessary for a student with special needs whose Individualized Education Plan (IEP) is being reviewed or an at-risk student who is under the close scrutiny of the student assistance team. At times like these, when you need to analyze student work samples in order to provide a complete description of what a student can and cannot do, underwriting comes in very handy.

- Student journals can be used at parent-teacher conferences to show a student's current abilities in writing as well as the progress that he or she has made over the past few months. It is quite difficult to recall exactly what a student with very basic skills was trying to write on a particular day without the help of underwriting. If you cannot clearly show parents what a student was attempting to write, then you cannot very easily communicate what the individualized mini-lesson may have been for the student that day and how this and other mini-lessons are used to move the student along in his or her writing development.

- Students' writing will be published later in the school year, as explained in Chapter 4, and it will be helpful to have an accurate record of what a student wrote before it is typed and made into a book. Because some students' writing will become quite lengthy by springtime, it will serve you well to use underwriting for any word that is not readable or any sentence that does not make sense on its own.

- If there is no underwriting on a student's journal pages when they are sent home, it will be tough for a parent to know what his or her child was trying to write and therefore make it less likely that the parent will make a positive and specific comment to the child. For instance, when there is no underwriting a parent might not realize that the *c* on her child's journal page, which appears to be just a random letter, is actually a well-thought-out representation for the word *see*—an accomplishment to celebrate.

You will be writing on students' papers often with this approach as a means of enhancing your teaching points, so your underwriting should not cause dismay. If it does, or if students ask what you are writing, all you need to say is, "You wrote down the sounds you can hear, just like you were supposed to; this is just another way to write it." Or, you might tell students that the teacher's writing will be helpful to them or others who try to read their writing.

While it is important for students not to focus on a teacher's underwriting, there is no need to write tiny, sideways, or in cursive to try to hide the correct spelling of a word or make the underwriting less obvious. In fact, writing the word correctly just above or below the student's attempt at the word (wherever there is room), in neat lowercase letters, might result in the student examining it closely and either memorizing the word or referring back to it on another occasion when he or she wants to write the same word. Since the ultimate goal is for students to use conventional spelling, then students should not be discouraged from looking at your underwriting in order to spell a word correctly. Rather, the child's resourcefulness should be celebrated.

Yasmin, age 5 Note that the student erased her original writing and replaced it by copying the teacher's underwriting. Students rarely do this, but if it does happen explain right away that she needs to keep her original writing because you really need to see how she wrote the words to best be able to teach her. However, if she wants to use your teacher-written words in a new piece of writing, she can look back at this page.

Circulating for the Third Time/Closure

It is important to establish a method of bringing the writing session to a close for each student on an individual basis, just as it was essential during the first six weeks of school to help students feel closure daily. As before, putting stars on the students' papers is a way to signal to them that they performed well, did what you expected, and therefore are finished for the day. More important, the lack of a star on a journal paper reminds you that a student still needs some feedback and help getting to closure.

Upon completing your second trip around the room, at least half of the students should be finished, meaning they have stars on their papers, and the remaining students should be nearing completion of implementing the SO part of their individualized mini-lessons. A quick glance at the students' journal pages, to look for the star or other sign of being finished, will assist you in determining which students you need to see in the third round. You can also just ask the class, "Who still needs a star?" There will be some students who do not have a good sense of time or pacing themselves, and for them, it may be necessary to make an announcement such as, "There

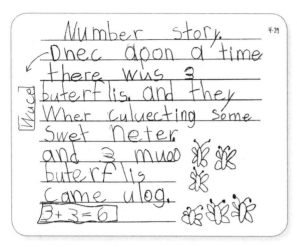

Kyle, age 5 I wanted Kyle to spell the word *once* correctly by recalling some recent instruction about it and by using the resources available in the classroom. I provided a practice box in which Kyle was to write the correct spelling. I failed to follow up and the word was never spelled correctly, hindering the type of closure that furthers understanding.

are two minutes left for journal writing. If you don't have a star yet, you have two minutes to finish."

Generally, the third time around the room takes three to five minutes. At this point, if any student is requiring more than 20 or 30 seconds of individualized assistance, it may be best to quickly model, right there on the student's journal page, what needs to be done, rather than continuing to wait and see if the student is going to be able to do it. The modeling will serve as an individualized mini-lesson and will be effective as long as the modeling does not occur with the same student day after day and does not discourage the student's independence and resourcefulness. Also, try to avoid going past the time allotted for writing (there are other very important things to do in a kindergarten day), but do strive to make sure each and every student gains closure each and every day. It may take a few days, as it did with the whole-group drawing and writing lessons, to learn how your students pace themselves as well as how to pace yourself.

When all students have gained closure and journal writing time has ended, indicate to students that they should carefully close their journals and put them away.

MEETING THE NEEDS OF NEW STUDENTS

Because of the structure and format of daily writing, it is possible to take students at any level and involve them in your daily writing time, including new students who arrive in your classroom at any point in the school year.

Chances are, if a student joins your class later in the school year, he or she may not have participated in six weeks of daily guided writing at his or her previous school. The opportunity to write in a daily journal may not have been available and many of the skills you introduced during the first six weeks of school, as well as what the students have learned through their daily individualized mini-lessons, could very well be foreign to the new student. Fortunately, the ability to hold a pencil and make marks on a piece of paper is about all that is required for a child to participate in journal writing time and for you to begin scaffolding your instruction.

Because the writing routine in your classroom is so well-established and your students will be so engrossed in what they are doing, a new student will have little choice but to join in and attempt to write. As the new student watches the other students to see what they are doing, he or she will most likely draw a picture and then attempt to write some letters, just as the other students do. As you circulate about the room, you will deliver individualized mini-lessons to this student, meeting the student right where his or her skills are and determining the pace at which he or she will be able to progress. During the many years that this approach has been in use, students have often joined the class as late as the spring and were, like most of the other students, capable of writing a set of readable and related sentences by the end of the school year. If anything, this method encourages new students to jump right in and write alongside their peers. Once they are writing on a daily basis and benefiting from individualized mini-lessons, most will exhibit steady progress.

SKILLS ASSESSMENT

There are three major areas to assess during this part of the school year (approximately December or January):

- knowledge of letter names and sounds
- reading back one's own writing
- the stage of spelling development

Knowledge of Letter Names and Sounds

Kindergarten students are typically assessed on their knowledge of letter names (capital and lowercase) and sounds. These assessments can provide a valuable picture of how a student is progressing and what difficulties he or she may encounter in the future in both reading and writing. The implementation of daily writing should have a noticeable and positive impact on the rate at which students learn letter names and sounds. Any concern you have about this—especially if it is your first year to not directly and systematically teach the letters of the alphabet one at a time—should be allayed once you compile the results of this assessment.

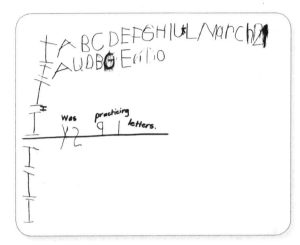

Ruby, age 6 This student was new to the class in the spring and arrived with little knowledge of the alphabet. She was quick to notice that the other students were putting letters all over their papers and mimicked them by finding a classroom alphabet to copy. The *I* at the beginning of her lines may indicate that she observed nearby students' writing sentences beginning with the word *I*. Her comment, "I was practicing letters" served as a springboard for an individualized mini-lesson, in which I helped Ruby write this sentence by sounding out, naming, and recording the corresponding letters.

Reading Back One's Own Writing

While students are first learning the process of formulating and writing sentences on their own, an important skill to help them develop is the ability to read back what they have written. The goal is for a student to realize that the letters he or she put upon the paper represent the idea that was in his or her head before and while it was written. The student should be able to point to any actual words that are on the paper and read them back. Or, if the student is in the stage of spelling development in which he or she still writes random letters, you would watch for the student to move his or her finger across the page from left to right and tell what idea the letters represent.

This skill will come quite naturally to most students if it has been modeled daily during the first six weeks of school. As demonstrated in Chapter 2, you have been modeling from the very first lesson how to read and reread what has been written on the page to ensure that it represents the intended thought or sentence. Also, if activities and lessons that help students to learn sight words and voice-print match are occurring at other times during the kindergarten day, then students should be able to point to the words and read what was written. A student need not demonstrate perfect reading or voice-print match to pass this assessment; rather, look for an understanding by the student that the written words represent the student's idea.

This skill is best assessed while you circulate about the room during writing time. Whether officially assessing students on their ability to read back their writing or just giving individualized mini-lessons, a useful and common inquiry is, "What did you write today? Can you read it to me?" Most students will eagerly and proficiently read back what they have written. When you observe this on several consecutive days, mark these students off as having mastered the skill. A checklist will help you narrow your attention to those students who still need assistance with this skill.

If a student tells you, "I don't know what it says" or "I don't know how to read," teach an individualized mini-lesson for that student about how writing is the student's idea or the student's talking written down on paper. Remind the student about the topic for the day or look closely at the student's drawing and comment that it is obvious from his drawing that he or she must have written about something related to the topic. Explain that writers know what they've written because the words on the paper show their ideas and they have done the writing. Say that you are going to come back in a few minutes and you want the student to be ready to tell you what he or she wrote about. All you will expect from the student at this point is to repeat the topic for the day or, even better, to tell you a sentence related to the topic of the day. Initially, it will not be appropriate for this student to point and read since he or she does not yet understand that writing carries meaning or that it represents the writer's idea. Continue with this focus for the student's individualized mini-lessons, scaffolding your instruction and expectations appropriately, and the student will soon learn that his writing has meaning and can be explained or read to others.

The Stages of Spelling Development

Every kindergarten teacher should have a good understanding of the stages of spelling development. When trying to determine in which stage a student is, consider only the letters and sounds a student records for words. Do not, at this time, look at spacing, letter formation, ideas, or any other aspect of the student's writing. It is also best to analyze a considerable amount of student writing, or a series of journal entries, when determining a student's stage of spelling development, so you have a true picture of the student's skills.

A description of each stage, based on the work of Richard Gentry (2000), and a kindergarten sample from the first four stages are shown on the following pages.

Stage 1: Random Letter Spelling

Student writes random letters, numbers, other symbols, or even squiggles; no obvious sound-letter correspondence.

Genevieve, age 5 This student is in the random letter stage of spelling development.

Stage 2: Partially Phonetic Spelling

Student writes one or more, but not all, sound(s) heard in each word; writing may include some extra letters as well.

Sherwood, age 5 Sherwood's writing is partially phonetic.

Stage 3: Phonetic Spelling

Student writes most sounds heard in each word; spells by ear; includes vowels but not necessarily the correct vowels; writing is readable.

Ashley, age 6 This writing sample shows classic Stage 3 phonetic writing.

On spring brayk, my mom gayv me a bicke lesen because I am lurnnihg to ride a too weler. First my mom hellped me then I tryd it by my sellf and my mom wocht me then my mom sed good Job. then my mom got an her bicke and I wocht her

Michaela, age 5 Michaela's writing shows many examples of transitional spelling, in which she applies, but may overgeneralize, spelling rules: **1.** using *-ing*, *-er*, and *-ed* endings; **2.** using a silent *e* or common vowel combinations, such as *ay*, when writing words with long vowels, such as *break* and *gave*; **3.** doubling the consonant that follows a short vowel sound in words like *helped* (*hellped*) and *myself* (*my sellf*); and **4.** using a vowel before the *r* in the words *learning* and *first*.

Stage 4: Transitional Spelling

Student starts to apply spelling rules and use letter chunks and endings; relies more on visual aspects and memory of words than the sounds that can be heard.

Stage 5: Conventional Spelling

Student spells most words correctly. Students generally reach this stage during their late elementary years.

When familiarizing yourself with these stages or explaining them to parents, it is helpful to take one word, such as *phone*, and think about how students in each of the five different stages of spelling development might write it.

Stages of Spelling Development for *Phone*

Stage 1	Random Letter Spelling	squiggles	*eoxo*		
Stage 2	Partially Phonetic Spelling	*f*	*febs*	*n*	*fn*
Stage 3	Phonetic Spelling	*fon*			
Stage 4	Transitional Spelling	*fone*	*phon*	*fown*	
Stage 5	Conventional Spelling	*phone*			

Circulating among your students daily during writing time, all the while carefully studying the students' writing for the most appropriate and most timely teaching points, will give you a very good idea of which stages of spelling development your students are in. It will be quite easy to determine whether students are still writing random letters, whether they are including just a few sounds for most words, if they are able to hear all the phonemes in words and record the correct letters for them all, or if they are moving into the transitional stage of spelling as indicated by their words' being more visually correct. To determine a student's stage of spelling development, be sure to assess the way in which the student writes words at a time when you are sure he or she has not copied a neighbor's paper or listened to another student elongate the sounds or tell which letters to write. Also, at least 50 percent of a student's writing has to fall into a certain category in order for the student to be considered as being at that stage of spelling development (Gentry, 2000).

Because they've participated in six weeks of whole-group guided writing with phonemic segmentation practice, most students will skip altogether the random letter stage of spelling and will demonstrate partially phonetic or phonetic spelling upon starting independent writing in October. If you are aware of your students' stage of spelling development and approximately how long they have been in their current stage, then you can more easily make decisions about the degree and timing of instructional support necessary to move them into the next level of spelling. While there is no set standard, except for the fact that most kindergarten curricula expect partially phonetic spelling by the end of the year, it is fair to expect most students to be strong phonetic spellers by January and, depending on whether you explicitly teach a variety of word endings and letter chunks, several might display some transitional spelling by May. Though the conventional stage of spelling development is mentioned here, it is rare for students of this age to spell enough words correctly to be considered conventional spellers.

Writing Scoring Rubric

A helpful tool for you and your students at this point in the school year is a scoring rubric that establishes a uniform set of precisely defined criteria or guidelines for assessing students' writing and for supporting instruction. Using a rubric is practical and effective whenever you need to let students know up front exactly what is being expected of them, objectively evaluate student writing, and/or provide feedback to students and parents about how, specifically, students can improve their writing.

The writing scoring rubric shown on page 92 was developed exclusively for the kindergarten classroom and includes descriptions for standard kindergarten proficiencies in the areas of:

- sound-letter correspondence
- spacing
- handwriting
- content and fluency
- sentence structure
- periods as end marks

Because kindergartners who learn through this daily writing approach tend to develop more advanced skills than are commonly expected for this grade level, and because all students should be encouraged to strive for higher levels of performance, there are also descriptors on the rubric that go above and beyond typical kindergarten targets for each of the six areas. This ensures that the rubric remains an effective assessment and teaching tool for all students, including those who are beyond where they are expected to be according to the curriculum.

MAKING SHORT TIME OF ASSESSMENT

After you become accustomed to the rubric, it will not take long to score a set of student writing samples, especially if you are in the habit of using underwriting and do not need to take the time to decipher students' writing during the scoring process.

Name _____

Date _____ Score _____

Kindergarten Writing Scoring Rubric

Target Score: 12 (at least 2 points in each of the six areas)

	0	1	2	3	4
	Developing Students scoring 0 or 1 need support to reach at least a 2 by May.		**Proficient** Writing meets curriculum expectations for the end of kindergarten.	**Above grade level**	**One or more grades above level**
Sound-letter correspondence	marks other than letters, or letters scattered on paper	random letters	partially phonetic; at least one (but not all) sounds included for most words with possibly a few random or wrong letters recorded	phonetic spelling; most sounds for most words; many sight words spelled correctly	transitional spelling; includes most sounds, endings, chunks; most sight words spelled correctly
Spacing	letters scattered on paper	linear letters, with left to right directionality; random or nonexistent spacing	most spacing correct; a few minor mistakes	visible spaces placed between words and none in the middle of words	all spaces placed correctly and evenly (not too big or too small)
Handwriting	no letters, letters touching, illegible writing, or too much erasing	most letters recognizable, but wrong size or case, or too much erasing	most letters formed correctly; may have wrong case, height, or reversals	only a few errors in case, height, formation; letters sit on perceived or actual line	handwriting is nearly perfect, with no obvious areas for improvement
Content and fluency	unable to verbalize what the writing is about	can verbalize what was written and/or pretends to read back the writing	knows topic; accurately reads back own writing with nearly correct voice-print match	writes more than one sentence; stays on topic; may repeat some ideas	fluent writing with at least three details about a topic or a beginning, middle, end; doesn't repeat
Sentence structure	no thoughts represented; no sentences	incomplete sentence(s) or run-on ideas	one complete sentence	two or more complete and grammatically correct sentences	complete, correct sentences, some with varied structure
Periods as end marks	no periods	_____	at least one period	more than one period; at least one in correct place	at least three periods in the correct places

Comments _____

Using the Rubric as an Assessment Tool

Looking at the rubric, you will see the six skill areas listed down the left side. Students earn 0 to 4 points for each subskill, depending on what they produce and demonstrate on their writing samples, ranging from below proficiency (0 or 1 point), proficient performance (2 points), and above-grade-level performance (3 or 4 points). Since a score of 2 is considered proficient based on most kindergarten curricula and the commonly accepted targets for kindergarten writing, the target is for students to earn at least 2 points in each area, or a total of 12 points, by the end of the year. Since this particular rubric allows students to earn additional points for demonstrating skills beyond the targeted levels and because students excel with this daily writing approach, you will find that by the end of the year, most students will earn more than 12 points.

The purpose of this rubric up until the month of March is mainly for you to assess student writing and gauge their progress. Students should not yet be aware of the rubric or of scores they obtain. In the spring, when students are a little more sophisticated, you will be able to introduce the rubric in sections and use it as a teaching tool in addition to using it for assessment purposes. The student writing samples and companion rubrics below show how the rubric can be used to objectively evaluate student writing.

Beginning in January, try to score at least one writing sample from each student for each of the remaining months of school. The scores themselves will serve two main purposes: 1) to determine how your class is doing as a whole and 2) to establish how students are doing individually and whether they are improving over time, as indicated by their initial and subsequent scores. In addition, the scores will assist you in reflecting upon your teaching.

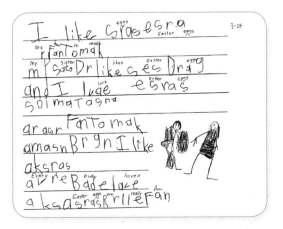

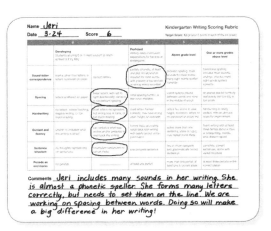

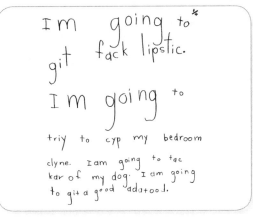

Using the Rubric as a Teaching Tool

A rubric is a powerful communication tool. It communicates in concrete and observable terms that which is valued most in the development of proficient kindergarten writing and helps clarify for parents, colleagues, and students what you are expecting and hoping to see demonstrated. Unlike older students, kindergartners will not be able to read or fully understand the descriptions as they are written on the rubric; they can, however, benefit from you showing them how many points they earned and telling them what they need to do in order to get more points next time. Students can then begin to critically evaluate their own work, a skill which will be indispensable for the rest of their lives.

The skills included on the rubric are listed in the order that they typically develop and begin to appear in students' writing as well as in the order of their importance according to most kindergarten curricula. For example, during journal writing time, the first skill you will model and thus the first skill students will demonstrate is the recording of letters on their papers. Once they are somewhat proficient at this, you should expect them to begin spacing between words. Proper letter formation must be taught and promoted at about this time, too; waiting until later in the year or until first grade for students to concern themselves with the appearance of their written work is almost always too late. When students have the first three skills in place, you can begin to expect more from them in the areas of content and sentence structure. Last, some kindergarten students will be ready to fully understand and make use of end punctuation in their writing.

When it comes time to introduce the scoring rubric to students, it is recommended that you present just one skill, or line, of the rubric at a time. Since the skills are listed in order of typical development as well as their significance for this age group, it makes sense to begin at the top of the rubric.

Choose a time other than daily journal writing time (or skip having students write one day and make use of the daily writing period) to present the scoring for one skill on the rubric. Tell your students that you recently scored some of their writing. Explain what this means by saying that you gave them some points for how well they wrote. They will want to know their scores, so reassure them that you will give them that information later. Show students only the portion of the rubric you're targeting. It is not necessary to enlarge it because they probably cannot read it or understand the descriptions at this point. Instead, briefly summarize the criteria for each skill category in a way students can understand. For example, you might explain the criteria for sound-letter correspondence in this way: "When I scored your writing, I was looking at how many sounds you put for each word you wrote and if you wrote the right letters for the sounds you heard. If it is still hard for you to hear sounds and write the matching letters, then you probably got one point. And we'll keep working on it. If you put down some good sounds, but you forgot to write *all* the sounds, then I gave you two points. For those of you who have almost all the sounds for all the words you wrote, you got three points. To get four or five points, you have to have good sounds *and* spell the words on the word wall correctly *and* use some of the chunks and endings that we've learned." Students will not take in all of this information and they do not need to at this time. All they need to understand is that you are looking closely at how they spell words.

When you get a chance, speak to students individually about their scores and discuss with them what they need to do to get higher scores. Only do the latter, however, if you feel the skill level needed to reach the next point value is within a student's immediate reach and if you are going to make a point of recalling how students scored and then assist them in trying to improve during daily writing time. If you tell students how to improve but do not provide the support they will need to do so, then they may begin to feel that the next step is unobtainable for them.

Repeat the process of introducing the remaining skills on the rubric, going over scores earned by students, and then using the rubric to explicitly teach students how to improve their writing, one subskill at a time. In this manner, the rubric becomes an excellent teaching tool to help students move along the continuum of learning. Practical suggestions for helping students improve in the separate areas on the rubric are included in the Skills Assessment section of Chapter 4, beginning on page 111.

If using a scoring rubric sounds like something you would like to try, but the rubric included here does not quite meet your needs, feel free to develop a rubric of your own, either by starting from scratch or by modifying this one. You may change the skills, the standard, or target scores for which you would like your students to strive, or the defined criteria for the varying point values for each skill. If you design your own rubric, be sure to test it out on several pieces of writing before recording or reporting scores obtained by its use. It will not work to score samples in December, modify your rubric somewhat based on some weaknesses discovered within it, score more writing in March, and then try to compare the scores between December and March. The only way to truly compare scores is to use the very same assessment tool.

COMMUNICATING WITH PARENTS

The information you provide to parents about the development of writing in young children can occur in a large group, such as Back-to-School Night or a Curriculum and Classroom Information Night, depending on the format and timing of such events, the amount of time you have, and the degree to which parents are ready to process such information; or, you can talk about it in a more intimate setting, such as parent-teacher conferences. By fall parent-teacher conference time, parents will have seen a number of writing samples come home. They realize that you value writing instruction in your classroom and have probably already seen quite a bit of growth in their child. Parents will be thrilled about their child's progress and equally excited about what will develop during the remainder of the school year.

The parent-teacher conference is a good time to take advantage of their interest level and quickly explain a little about writing development and instruction for young children so they understand where their child is with learning to write and, more importantly, where they are headed. Showing parents the criteria for each of the subskills on the rubric can help give them a more complete understanding of what goal their child is working toward in writing and how you are supporting his or her development to meet and exceed these grade-level goals.

Spelling is the most noticeable element of emergent writing and serves as a focal point in most of your conversations with parents. There are two important points to share with parents when discussing the stages of spelling development and when sharing writing samples. First, explain where their child is now and where you expect him or her to be by the end of the school year. You can base your expectations on what is outlined in your district's kindergarten writing curriculum, but it may be that the stages of spelling development are not discussed in the curriculum and/or there is not a comparable expectation delineated for you. If this is the case, use the common standard or benchmark for many kindergarten programs—that kindergarten students be at the partially phonetic stage of spelling development by the end of kindergarten and as they enter first grade.

Because of the up-front work you did with your students during the six-week period of guided journal writing, at this point in the school year several of your students may already be at or beyond the partially phonetic stage of spelling development. When explaining this to parents, it may be helpful to say, "According to the kindergarten curriculum [*or* according to the commonly accepted standard for kindergartners], your child should be a partially phonetic speller by May. Looking at his/her writing, we can see that he/she is already past that and is a phonetic speller. And there are still many months left in the school year."

The other important thing that parents need to understand is that students stay in the phonetic and transitional stages of spelling development for very long periods of time. Since most children's spelling is not considered conventional until late elementary or middle school, there will most likely be a period of several years when they are spelling phonetically and/or spelling by eye where they include common letter patterns, such as *-ing, kn-,* or *-tion,* but do not quite have the correct spelling for most words. Therefore, parents should not be overly concerned when their child's spelling development seems to slow down once they become consistently strong phonetic spellers. Students' spelling may look the same for a period of a year or more; during this time, however, they should show improvement in other areas of writing, such as spacing, letter formation, content and fluency, sentence structure, and the use of end punctuation.

Perhaps the best way to communicate to parents about spelling development is to display many student writing samples at school, which will provide examples of the different stages of spelling development. The paramount reason to display the writing is to allow parents to see what some of the other students in the class are doing and to make comparisons and conclusions of their own about their child's progress in writing.

IN REVIEW

These four months of independent and individualized writing instruction should have provided ample opportunity to differentiate instruction and encourage students to practice applying, at their individual levels, the various concepts and skills you have introduced thus far. The assessment data you have with regard to knowledge of letter names and letter sounds, along with your students' stages of spelling development, probably indicates that by January, many of your students are nearing or have surpassed the goals you had in mind for them for the end of their kindergarten year. And certainly the daily practice of reading back their own writing has had a tremendous effect not only on your students' writing ability but also on their overall reading development.

I am sure you may have a handful of students, as in all classes, who are not quite where you want them to be, and it will be important to provide extra support for them as you move forward to the next portion of the yearlong plan. In the meantime, celebrate the commitment you have made to individualizing daily writing instruction and the successes you and your students have experienced thus far.

Chapter Four

Independent Writing and Publishing: February–April

During this part of the school year, students' stamina, enthusiasm, and writing skills reach new heights through the publishing of their writing in books. According to the yearlong plan shown on page 9, writing instruction for these months will involve:

- Supporting students as they continue to write independently in their journals.

- Providing a daily topic for writing; students are encouraged to use the provided topic but also may use a topic of their own choosing.

- Teaching mainly through brief, individualized mini-lessons.

- Giving students the option of carrying writing over from one day to the next.

- Publishing student writing in books.

- Providing opportunities for students to illustrate, share, and read repeatedly the books they have written.

- Planning a celebration to recognize students' published works.

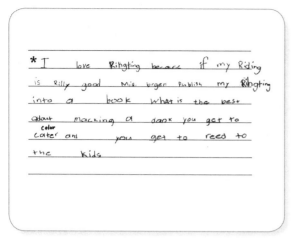

Merced, age 5

DAILY WRITING TIME

During the months of February, March, and April, daily writing time continues for the most part just as it has for the past four months. When the writing period begins, students listen for the topic of the day and begin writing. Maintain the process of circulating about the room, delivering individualized mini-lessons based on teaching points that arise from the students' writing. Most students will be able to write quite independently by this time of the year and will regularly be writing several sentences on their papers. Their sentences will be readable, meaningful, and incredibly sophisticated, in both ideas and skills. Because of this, you may begin to wonder what else you can possibly teach your students.

The goal of daily writing is to help students develop the ability and desire to skillfully and fluently write their ideas. This focus prepares students to easily and confidently move on to more advanced skills in future years. Therefore, it makes sense to continue to help students master beginning writing skills while improving their fluency and stamina so they can comfortably and enthusiastically write more and more as time goes on.

In order to keep the momentum and excitement about writing going and to provide you with new teaching points, the purpose of daily writing time will change slightly. Beginning in February and continuing through April, students will have the opportunity to have several writing samples published as books. It will not be necessary to change the format of daily writing time that has been established and in place since October. Nor will you need to create additional time for individual student conferences that are usually associated with getting student writing ready for publication. While the process of putting together books will definitely require some of your time each day, the overall effort needed is minimal and the tremendous effect it will have on student writing is well worth it.

OVERVIEW OF BOOK PUBLISHING

When February arrives, gather your students together for a quick explanation about publishing. It is helpful to have a read-aloud book as well as a sample student-published book for this, but the latter is not absolutely necessary. The books you publish for your students will have a construction paper cover and white sheets of paper inside upon which the students' words have been typed. The students will illustrate and color each page in their books. At the back of each book will be a photocopy of the students' actual writing, so that anyone who reads the book will understand that the book was indeed written by the student and not just dictated.

Begin the publishing talk with your students by making sure they understand how a real book gets published. You might want to do an entire unit on this by introducing an author and reading books or showing videos about the author, his or her work, and the process he or she went through to have a book published. Or, just talk briefly about the publishing process, explaining in simple terms what happens before a book ends in bound copy on a shelf. Some students will have never thought about or had an opportunity to talk about this process with anyone and will benefit from

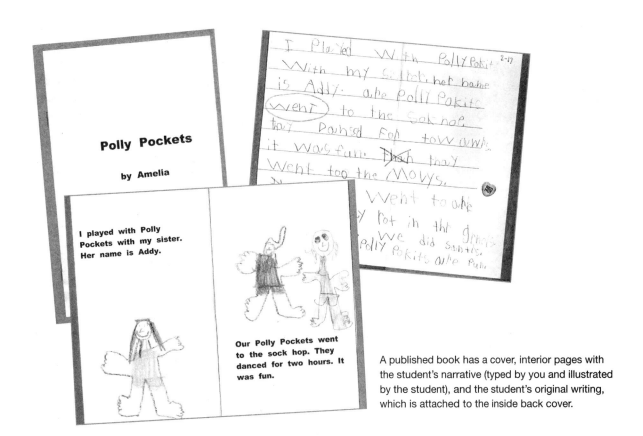

A published book has a cover, interior pages with the student's narrative (typed by you and illustrated by the student), and the student's original writing, which is attached to the inside back cover.

Polly Pockets

by Amelia

I played with Polly Pockets with my sister. Her name is Addy.

Our Polly Pockets went to the sock hop. They danced for two hours. It was fun.

this background information to fully understand the concept of publishing.

Next, tell your students that since they have become such wonderful writers, they are going to have their writing published as books. Be sure to explain and show what their published books will look like so they are not disappointed when they realize their books are not going to be illustrated by professional artists or typeset and bound by a printer. Most students' enthusiasm will hardly be affected by the difference between a book with a construction paper cover and student illustrations and the real book with which you compare it. For the students, what seems to be the most thrilling aspect of student-published books is that the words they wrote in their journals will now appear in a typed format with everything magically spelled correctly. This feature of the publishing process really makes students feel their writing is special.

To alleviate any concerns you may have about starting the process of publishing student writing, it is important to know that, in kindergarten, one sentence of writing may be all that is required to make a book. The books that are published will, for the most part, be two to five sentences long and therefore not require much teacher time to produce. This writing approach, including the publishing, was developed in a school that had half-day kindergarten sessions; that means each spring was spent publishing books for up to 52 students. If you have this many students, or more, you may decide to publish just a few books for each student. A teacher with fewer students may be able to publish four or more books for each student before the end of April.

Setting the Standards for Publication

Students need to understand that having their work published is a special honor and thus there will be some expectations and requirements that need to be met in order for it to occur. Although all students will not be able to meet this standard, and some will far exceed it, set the expectation that in order to get a book published, students must write at least three interesting sentences that go with the topic about which they are writing. Do a quick modeled writing lesson to demonstrate what you mean. Choose a topic that students will enjoy and begin writing. Be sure to think out loud as you write. You might say:

Sample Lesson: Writing Substantially on a Topic

"I'm so excited to get a book published. I think I'll write a book about my dog. Let's see, I have to tell at least three interesting things about my dog. I can do that because my dog is really important to me. Okay, here I go. I'll start by writing *I have a dog named Alice.*"

Write the first sentence, but don't worry about discussing sounds, spacing, or anything else. The purpose of the lesson is to show how to write at least three pleasing sentences about one topic.

Continue to think aloud and compose a second and third sentence: "I better tell what kind of dog she is so everyone who reads my book will know. *Alice is a golden retriever.* My dog is kind of wild, and she tears around the yard when we get home because she's so happy to see us. I think I'll write that. *My dog tears around the yard when we get home.*"

Review and write a final sentence to serve as a conclusion. "Let's see, how many things have I told about my dog? First, I said she was a golden retriever. Then I said she tears around the yard. I also told her name. That's three things. I'm almost done. I just want to say that I love my dog. My last sentence is: *I love my dog.*"

You will not be talking about conclusions and will not expect your students to include them in their writing, but it does not hurt to model an appropriate ending for your writing. Finish up by once again thinking aloud:

"I really like this story about my dog. I think it's ready for my teacher to publish."

Ask students if they think they can write three sentences about something interesting (of course they will think they can because you have been preparing them for this and most of them will have been doing something similar to this in their journals for the past few months). Then inform them that they can try writing a piece for publication the next time they have journal writing.

The standards you set, coupled with the students' eagerness to have their writing published, will result in students writing at a skill level far beyond our traditional expectations of kindergartners.

FACILITATING INDEPENDENT WRITING TIME

Naturally, the very next day every student is going to want you to take what they have written and publish it as a book. It will be necessary to balance the enthusiasm the students have for this new idea of getting their writing published with the expectations you have always had for writing time. Reiterate to students that the procedures for journal writing time remain the same. Students should come into the classroom, start writing in their journals about the topic that is provided, and do their best work while you circulate. There should be no real difference in what they do during writing time. Maintaining your system of circulating around the room to provide timely individualized mini-lessons will help the students to understand this and carry on as usual.

Selecting Writing to Publish

To maintain the publishing fervor that you have initiated, choose a few pieces written by students as soon as possible and get the publishing process underway. As you circulate during writing time each day, you will see some pieces developing that might be suitable to publish. It will be on the third time of moving about the room that you will make some final decisions about whether any student writing is worthy of publication. To help with this process, consider the following points:

- What is realistic for this student with regard to the standard of writing at least three interesting sentences about the provided topic? You should have a general idea whether each student will meet or exceed expectations, or need additional support or modifications in order to publish.

- Is one or two sentences more realistic? Adjust the expectation so that every student may participate in the publishing process, even if the result is a one- or two-sentence book.

- Is additional support necessary? Some students will benefit from you writing another sentence or two for them to make their story longer and more interesting. (Don't add too much; eventually this student will have to read the book.)

- Can the student write three simple pattern sentences instead? Remind a student that he can quickly and easily write a few more sentences that are similar to a first sentence. (Example: *I like dogs. I like cats. I like fish.*)

- How much time is required to meet the standard? Did a student use his time well but still only get two sentences done in 30 minutes? Was a student able to write three interesting sentences in just ten minutes? Should he or she then be expected to write more? The amount of time it takes and the effort put forth by a student to meet the standard can help you adjust your expectations.

- What has the student already published? Is the current piece more sophisticated in length, ideas, or format than the previous publications by this student? To ensure that students continue to go all out to be published, gradually raise your expectations with each publication.

The individualized mini-lesson for each student who is going to have that day's writing published should include:

- Having the student read his or her writing to you (you will have already read it on a previous trip around the room and made a mental note that it is probably suitable to be published),

- asking the student if he or she thinks this writing is ready to be made into a book, and

- quickly suggesting a few possible titles for the piece and letting the student make the final decision.

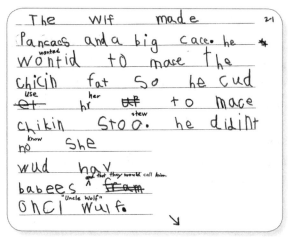

Andy, age 5 "Revision" of this piece consisted of talking to Andy and making a few minor changes to his writing so it would make sense as a published story.

Only a handful of students, while still in kindergarten, will reach the point in their writing development where you need to work on organization of content with them. The main goal with kindergarten students is to help them become fluent in getting one or more sentences down on paper. It is a real accomplishment for a student to write three sentences, even if he or she does it every day during journal writing time, and it should be celebrated rather than heavily edited. During the publishing months, however, it may be necessary with longer pieces to discuss the meaning and the organization of the content with a student, and together make some changes that will help readers more easily understand and enjoy the writing. It is easiest to take care of this while circulating during regular writing time, as was done with Andy's piece at left, because the writing will be fresh in the student's mind. For the most part, writing in kindergarten is mostly about first drafts and a little bit of editing. There is plenty of time to practice revision in later grades.

Maintaining a Publishing Pace

Choosing, on average, one to three pieces for publishing each day will help set and preserve a steady pace, for both you and the students. Once you learn the process of typing and constructing the published books, it will be quite easy to prepare a few of them each day on a steady basis. It works best to complete the typing and preparation of the book within the 24-hour period between the time you collect the student's journal and the next writing period. That way, no matter what your procedure for having the student illustrate the book, his or her journal will be returned and available for writing the next day. A steady routine of typing and assembling books will ensure that you will not get behind in the process and, more important, that students regularly get to the next steps of illustrating and sharing their work, which is absolutely necessary if the practice of publishing is to have the tremendous effect on improving student writing that it can. As students' writing is published, illustrated, and shared with the class, the feverish enthusiasm and effort put forth by students to get their first and subsequent books published will enliven writing time markedly during the months of February, March, and April.

Record Keeping

Establish a system for tracking the number and titles of books that have been published for each student. Such record keeping will help ensure that all students are publishing books at a regular pace. Because of varying student abilities and motivation levels, not everyone will necessarily publish an equal number of books. If there are students in class who seem to have a piece ready for publication every few days, and you are able to keep up the pace of getting books typed and assembled, then, by all means, those students should have several (between five and ten) published books by the end of April. Other students, however, may not be as motivated or they may not be capable of meeting your expectations for improved writing in subsequent books and will take more time to write something worthy of publication. Set a minimum number of books each student should have so there is plenty to share and celebrate with parents at the upcoming author celebration. Your record keeping will allow you to zero in on those students who are not having their writing published often enough and who need a little extra support in order to have three books done in time for the big event.

Releasing Responsibility to Students

Not only will you see tremendous growth in your students' writing skills as the year goes on, but you will also witness dramatic changes in their ability to manage themselves, their writing, and their time. These changes will in turn affect how you manage independent writing time.

Allowing Choice of Writing Topics

So far during writing, students have been expected to write about daily topics that you have chosen carefully. This works well because it is motivating for students to write about subjects they typically would not choose on their own. Additionally, it is effective because the selected ideas often prompt students to include certain words or spelling patterns that you want the students to practice. As the school year progresses, however, and especially during the publishing months, students may wish to write about topics that are more timely and personally significant. Use your best judgment in deciding whether to allow a student to write about a topic he or she suggests; in most instances, it will be completely appropriate and worthwhile to have the student proceed with the idea. The continued practice of choosing and writing about topics other than those provided by you should be permitted as long as the topics promote steady growth and progress in the student's writing. If, for example, a student wants to write about a new puppy day after day and writes the same few sentences day after day, the student needs to go back to writing about the teacher-provided topics.

Carrying Writing Over to Subsequent Days

In addition to wanting to choose their own topics, students may also realize that sometimes it is necessary to carry over topics to successive days. The notion of doing this may have come up during previous months, but if not, it will definitely surface during the months of February, March, and April. Students will discover that in order to write in full about a topic or finish a piece they started they may need to write about it for more than one day, as was the case with Amy's piece about her loose tooth at right. When you see the need, begin each writing period with, "Today we are writing about _____; or, you may choose your own topic or continue to write about something that you started on a different day."

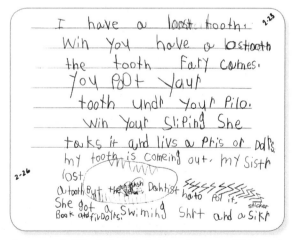

Amy, age 6 This student started her piece on a Friday and continued working on it the following Monday.

Tapering Student Support

As the end of the school year approaches, students will not require quite as much feedback and help with closure as was necessary in previous months. In fact, it is a good time to begin weaning the students from these once-vital components of daily writing time, such as checking for completion. Do not abandon students suddenly and completely, or the quality of their writing will surely diminish, but do change slightly the level and frequency of support. This will begin to prepare them for first grade, when their teacher may want them to work more independently and might not be checking with them two or three times during each session of writing.

THE PROCEDURE FOR PUBLISHING STUDENT BOOKS

There are many ways that classroom published books can be constructed, but this method is particularly suitable and results in a nice-sized, sturdy book that holds up well even with repeated readings.

Typing a Book

These steps outline how to format a new document into which you will type the sentences for a book.

1. Open a word processing program and set the page layout to the horizontal (landscape) orientation.

2. Go under *Format* and choose *Columns*. Set the whole document to be formatted in two columns.

3. Choose a large font, such as **Arial Black**.

4. Set the point size similar to that shown above (24 points).

5. Choose center justification for the first column on the first page of the document. Press the enter key until the cursor is approximately one-third of the way down the left column. Type the title of the book, press return, and type the word *by* followed by the first and last name of the student who wrote the book. If a student has rewritten or retold a story, you may prefer to write *retold by* rather than just *by* before the author's name. Always use two spaces between each word you type. This will help students discriminate between words when they read the final published product.

6. Hit the enter key as many times as it takes to get the cursor to the top of the right hand column. Each column you type will end up being one page in the finished book.

7. The top of the right-hand column is where you will begin typing the sentences the student wrote. Choose a slightly smaller font size, such as 20 points. For longer pieces, you may want to go as small as 14 points and type several sentences on each page.

8. Change the justification from center to left.

9. At the top of the column, type the first sentence the student wrote. As you go, correct the spelling (and wording, if needed to clarify the meaning) and add in any needed conventions, such as punctuation and capitalization. If the student's piece has only one sentence, go to Step 11.

I made a snowman and two snowflakes.	**Well, I couldn't finish it because I had to go home.**
Artwork **by Isabela**	
I glued some stuff on the snowman.	**When I was about to go Mrs. Bergen said, "You can finish it tomorrow."**

The two-column format allows you to fold the pages in half so they create a sturdy page printed on both sides.

10. Push the enter key until a second page is created in the document. You may choose to type the next sentence at the top of the left hand column or continue pushing enter until the cursor is near the bottom of the page in the left column. It works well to put some of the text at the top of the pages and some at the bottom and, with longer pieces, to vary the number of sentences you put on each page. The reading skills of the author may play a part in how and where you place the text.

    To aid students in properly illustrating their books, type at least one sentence per page for which an obvious accompanying picture can be drawn. Use the enter key as many times as needed to get to new columns and new pages. Most typed books will require three or fewer printed sheets of paper; if a book is longer than this, consider combining some sentences so fewer pages are needed.

11. Proofread your typing and check the placement of text all at the same time by going to *Print Preview* under *File.* If you are satisfied with the way it looks, print one copy of the entire book.

12. Print an additional copy of the page with the title and author information. You will use this for the book's cover.

13. Save the document and give it a general name such as *Published Book.* You may, for some reason, need to reprint what you just typed; the main reason to save it, however, is so that the next time you have to type a book you can open up this one and just replace the text that is there with the next student's writing. This will save you time formatting a new document.

14. Make two photocopies of the student's actual written piece from his or her journal. You may need to choose a darker setting on the copy machine for the pencil to show up. It does not matter if the copy is too dark, too light, or not very clean; it just needs to be readable. One copy will be sent home and the other will be included in the final published book.

Assembling a Book

The steps below explain how to quickly assemble a book. Once you have made a couple of books and have the hang of it, it will take less than two minutes to put each one together.

1. Choose one sheet of 9-by-12-inch construction paper. Any color will do but selecting a color that coordinates with the subject matter of the book is a nice touch. Fold the construction paper in half to make a book cover that is 6 by 9 inches.

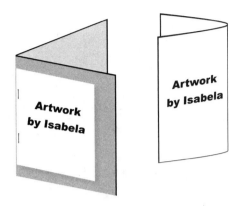

2. Take one of the papers that has the title information on it and fold it in half between the columns. Fold it back and forth a few times and crease it really well with your fingernail. Tear the sheet in half (or cut it in half) on the fold. Dispose of the half that has the first sentence on it and keep the half with the title and author information.

3. Use a glue stick to glue the half sheet of paper with the title information to the front of the construction paper book cover. Do not center it; rather, glue it slightly to the left, so that when the book is stapled together the half sheet with the title information will get caught in the staples and be more secure.

4. Find the other sheet from the printer that has the title on it and fold this sheet in half between the columns with the text showing on the outside when it is folded.

5. If there are additional sheets with story text, fold them in the same manner, with the text showing on the outside once the paper is folded. Since the pages are double thick, the student has the option of using markers to color the illustrations without worrying about the color showing through and making the lines of text on the next page difficult to read.

6. Put the open edges of the pages facing into the binding, with the title page first and the rest of the pages following in the correct order. Slip these pages inside the construction paper book cover, center them between the top and bottom of the cover, and staple them in place by putting two staples all the way through the construction paper front and back covers about one-half inch in from the left folded edge. Try to catch the paper that was glued to the front of the book, as well.

7. Open the book to each page, pressing creases against the stapled edge. Doing this will better enable the student to keep the book open while illustrating and reading it.

Attaching a Photocopy of the Original Writing

Take these steps to attach a photocopy of the student's actual writing from his or her journal to the inside back cover of the book.

1. Trim around a photocopy of the student's actual writing, cutting away approximately ½ inch from each 8 ½-inch edge of the paper so it will fit easily inside the edges of the construction paper cover when folded.

2. Using a glue stick, apply glue only to the right half of the back of the paper. Attach the sticky half of the paper to the inside of the back construction paper cover. Fold the left half over onto the right half that has been glued down (the writing will be on the inside of the fold), making sure the folded piece fits inside the creased area between the construction paper back cover and the last typed page of the book. Leave the left half of the paper flapping loosely; do not glue it to anything.

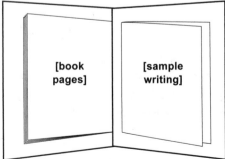

3. If the student's writing went onto a second or even third page, do Steps 1 and 2 with the last page the student wrote, and then repeat these steps for the previous pages. For example, with a piece that is written on three pages, start by gluing the right side of the back of the third page of the student's writing to the inside back cover. Next, glue the right side of the back of the second photocopied page from the student's writing onto the left side of the back of the third page, accordion style. Repeat this process to attach the first page of the student's writing to the second page. The pages with the student's writing will seem a little loose and floppy when you are finished, but that is how they need to be in order to help the book close more easily.

On the remaining photocopy of the student's writing, write a quick note to the parents, such as, "Congratulations! This writing will be published as a book." Send the copy home. This will continue your commitment to keeping parents informed of their children's progress. The student will be able to promptly share with his family the beginnings of a published book and receive positive attention and feedback for this work.

Illustrating a Book

After the book is typed and assembled, provide time for the student to illustrate it. This can happen during journal writing time at a special table set with crayons and markers, for any students who are illustrating their books. Or, students can sit among their classmates and illustrate and color. While coloring can be distracting to those who are writing in their journals, it can also serve as a great motivator for students to work hard and get published.

Before giving a freshly typed and assembled book to a student to be illustrated, it is best to give the author an opportunity to discuss, with an adult, the drawings he or she might include on each page of the book. Since this is a brand-new activity for kindergarten students, they may not understand that the picture on each page needs to correspond with the text on that page, and that they should do their best work first by drawing with a pencil and then adding color. You must teach these concepts and make these expectations clear.

There are several ways to accomplish this. First, you may want to gather the whole class together, have a student read his or her newly typed book, and then start a discussion as to what illustrations the author might include on each page. This doubles as a lesson on the importance of picture clues in books. Students will be eager to see if the author follows through and actually includes in his or her drawings some of the things the group suggests, which makes a great follow-up lesson. Another approach is to have a parent volunteer, senior volunteer, or instructional aide take the student one-on-one for a few minutes and to go over what might be included in the illustrations. If you have a large class and have found it necessary to have only three-fourths of your students writing each day (as described in the section on grouping students, in Chapter 3), then sharing published books and discussing illustration possibilities is a good activity for the remaining one-quarter of the students to do, assuming there is an adult working with them. No matter the method, be sure to provide explicit instruction to your students on how and why to illustrate their books with care.

Sharing Published Books

Once a student's writing is typed and assembled into a book and the book has been illustrated, the student must have an opportunity to share his or her work with the class. A whole-group setting is appropriate as all students, not just the author, will truly benefit from the experience. You could do this during your usual shared reading time or perhaps during the last few minutes of each day. It will soon become one of the students' favorite times of the day.

Most students will be able to read the books they have written quite well but you should be nearby to ensure students read accurately and do not just tell what the book says. It works well if you hold the book while the student reads, since adult hands are better able to hold a book open flat so the audience can see the illustrations. Also, if you hold the book you can better control the pace at which the book is read and take the time to point out an interesting choice of words, the way the student explained something in the book, or the care that was taken with the illustrations. Or you may prefer to have the student hold the book and learn to slowly and steadily show the illustrations after reading each page. Encourage the class to applaud when the student has finished reading the book.

The highlight—and the most effective aspect—of the sharing experience happens next. Once students realize what happens after the applauding, they will anticipate and relish this part more than the actual sharing of the book or the applause that follows. As the applause dies down, slowly turn to the pages of original writing in the back of the published book and say, "Did Jason *really* write this book? Yes, he did! And here is his writing to prove it!" This confirmation that the student did indeed write the book, when done consistently each time a student shares a published book, is what seems to inspire students in the audience, as well as the author, to write another book or a longer or better book. This is why it's so important to take the additional step of affixing a photocopy of the student's original journal writing in the back of his or her book.

Nothing will create such a sense of accomplishment, pride, and purpose for writing as standing before one's peers while they actively observe and listen to how words and illustrations come together in a book. The author of the published work will experience not only a sense of accomplishment in writing, but also in reading as he or she is able to read a book aloud that is probably more meaningful and has more word variety than any other book he or she typically reads. Sharing published books will become one of the students' favorite times of the day, whether they are sharing their own work or just enjoying books that have been created by their classmates. And the effect this has on developing students' passion for writing will make the time you devote to it well worth it.

The Accumulation of Published Books

As the system for publishing and sharing books becomes a routine part of the school day, you will find that you need a plan for what to do with all the books. For teachers who really get into the publishing process, it may well be that in the end there are close to 200 published books. There will be an author celebration night toward the end of April, so the books should remain in the classroom and, until then, undisclosed to the majority of parents. It would be a shame if, after a book was shared with classmates, it was put away until the celebration. On the other hand, because the books are so precious, you will need to establish a system that allows students to read the books without damaging or misplacing them. The books may be displayed in a particular part of the room with limited access. Invite students to read these books at times when the teacher or another adult can supervise the use of them, such as when an aide or other adult works with the rotating group. To be able to watch the published books accumulate on a shelf or bulletin board is highly rewarding and motivating to the students; surely, this is one of the purposes of going through the process of publishing books for students.

One system that works particularly well is to have students store their published books in plastic gallon-sized bags and provide them with many opportunities during the week to read the books. Encourage students to share their books by reading them to one another. I often hear students saying to their peers, "And did I *really* write this book? Yes, I did! Here's my writing to prove it." Ultimately, each author and owner is responsible for his or her own books, so if any book is lost or damaged it is the responsibility of the student to find it or initiate a way to have it repaired. Students will continue to be excited about rereading their books, especially when you remind them that they should practice so they can read the books to their families on the night of the author celebration.

In addition to preparing for the author celebration, there is another reason students should have the opportunity to read their published books repeatedly. These student-written books can serve as very appropriate reading material for kindergartners and should be used as one of the many different types of texts available to increase students' reading skills. A published book is a permanent record of a student's experiences or ideas, recorded in his or her own words. In this way, it is similar to the classic and highly effective Language Experience Approach (Stauffer, 1980) to teaching reading.

In a Language Experience Approach lesson, a student tells a story while the teacher records it on paper. The teacher writes it exactly as the student says it, whether the language and grammar are as precise as they should be or not. Once the story is recorded, the student can practice reading it and is generally quite successful because the text is highly predictable. If, in a class of 25 students, you have published an average of four books per student, then that is equivalent to recording 100 Language Experience Approach stories. This incredible wealth of reading material should not go to waste. Instead, students should have the opportunity to read and reread their published books on numerous occasions so they can not only continue to celebrate their writing but can also simultaneously improve their reading skills.

AUTHOR CELEBRATION NIGHT

The culmination of three months of publishing student writing is the author celebration event. This occasion should be held in the evening, with ample notification and advertisement, so that as many parents as possible can attend. While it seems that no parent would miss the opportunity to view and share in the excitement of the published work of his or her child, keep in mind that families have not been fully a part of the daily publishing zeal and may not be aware of how truly celebratory it is. Scheduling the event to coincide with other important happenings at the school may improve attendance. As the date for the event nears, you may wish to send home personalized invitations that list the titles of each student's books. The invitation should state that the parents will be able to take the keepsake books home with them following the big event. Although any family that does not attend will eventually get the published books, you may imply on the invitation that in order to procure them one must attend and celebrate the authors.

Why not hold the author celebration night in May, closer to the end of the school year? February, March, and April are the best months for students to work on having books published, and it is vital to invite family members to commemorate the book publishing soon after it reaches its climax in mid-April. To begin publishing later than February results in students getting a little bored with the same routine that has been happening since October and hampers their developing skills.

On the other hand, to start publishing in February and continue with it for four months, through the month of May, instead of wrapping it up in April, has a similar effect. Students lose their enthusiasm for publishing and may not be as proud of and thrilled with their books if the big event seems too far off. Also, it will be taxing for you to make time in your day for three straight months to type and assemble books; to persist with this for an even longer period of time would be burdensome and something to which you might not want to commit the following year. Furthermore, the month of May is already packed with school activities; to schedule yet another event during that time may result in limited attendance.

Hosting the Author Celebration

Most of the preparation for the author celebration night is completed in advance. Once the books have been published and the invitations sent home, there is little left to do. You and your students may wish to make refreshments available at the event; after all, what is a celebration without a few cookies? On the afternoon before families are expected to arrive, put the published books out on tables in the classroom, in no particular order. The books should be spread apart and placed in a manner that encourages people to glance at the various titles and drawings that are on the covers. In other words, it is important to mix them up and to not have all of one student's books together on the same table. To see all of the books displayed at once will be awe-inspiring. Having each student and his or her family hunt for the books will require them to glance at all the books, making the excitement of the process last longer for the student. Advertising the event as an open-house format will prevent all families from arriving at the same time. This will allow you to more easily greet and visit with the families as they come into the classroom.

When a family arrives, suggest they walk about the room, browsing through the books and picking up those that belong to their child. Once they have located all the titles their child has written, they can find a quiet spot in the room or the hall and sit down and listen to the author read the books. Some parents may not realize that this step—listening to their child read the books—needs to happen in order for the event to be as purposeful as it can be. Suggest to the parents that they listen to their child read his or her books to them and see how the book looks with all the illustrations. Unless you have incorporated other happenings into the author celebration night, the families are free to go after they have listened to their children read the books and, of course, enjoyed some refreshments. Be sure to remind parents to keep the published books forever so the students can look back on them in years to come.

SKILLS ASSESSMENT

The six areas on the Kindergarten Writing Scoring Rubric on page 92—spelling, spacing, handwriting, content and fluency, sentence structure, and periods as end marks—represent the skills to be assessed during this point in the school year. You may want to use the rubric to score a February writing sample for each student to determine areas of proficiency and difficulty. As explained in the Skills Assessment section in Chapter 3, students should score at least two points to be considered proficient in any given subskill. This expectation is for May, but it is necessary to start zeroing in on areas of weakness now in order to guide students toward full proficiency by the end of the year. Also, you can compare each student's January and February subskill scores, or just think about their writing in general, to determine if some of your students, though perhaps proficient, are not steadily improving and moving forward in certain areas. For those students who are not yet proficient, or for those who are proficient but are not showing continued growth, use some of the strategies explained in each section below to support them and to bring them along in the areas in which they need to improve.

Spelling Development

The different levels of spelling development are outlined on the scoring rubric in the *sound-letter correspondence* row. A thorough discussion of spelling development, along with examples of student writing at each level, begins on page 88.

By February, many students will be strong phonetic spellers and their writing will be quite readable. Others will be in the partially phonetic stage of spelling development and a few will be entering the transitional stage. Any students who are writing random letters at this point in the school year are probably new to the class or have been identified, either formally or informally, as having learning difficulties. This does not, however, mean that these students cannot and should not be expected to become partially phonetic spellers. There are still several months left in the school year and daily individualized mini-lessons should result in nearly all students eventually showing progress. The key is to keep your expectations high, to try novel approaches with these students, to supplement writing instruction outside of daily writing time, and to help students make connections between their writing and other classroom literacy activities.

One way to improve students' ability to hear and record sounds for words is to restore their use of putting up fingers for the sounds they hear, as described in Chapter 2, and then insist that they use this, or another similar, concrete method for segmenting and counting sounds. Sometimes partially phonetic spellers tend to drop the practice of this physical strategy at this point in the year (probably because most of their peers are no longer visibly displaying its use and you are not modeling it to the class as frequently as you once were), even though they really should be relying on it to progress toward more phonetic spelling.

Comparing students' stages of spelling development over the course of several months will highlight those students who are not steadily growing and improving. If, for example, a student has demonstrated phonetic spelling for several consecutive months with no signs of moving into the transitional stage of spelling, then you will want to give extra encouragement to help him or her start using common letter chunks, word endings, and other visual aspects of words that have been introduced. Despite having already met grade-level expectations, this student should receive the same amount of attention and expectation to move along and make progress in his or her writing skills as those students who are not quite where they need to be.

You can gather more teaching ideas by reading the student writing samples and accompanying individualized mini-lessons in the sound-letter correspondence section of Chapter 6, pages 129–131.

Spacing

A student's ability to properly space between words usually develops concurrently with spelling. This is especially true if you emphasized spacing during the six weeks of modeled and guided journal writing, and if you check that students use it consistently in their independent journal writing.

The standard expectation for kindergarten is that students will put a space between most words while writing. In order to do this, students need to have a well-developed concept of what constitutes a word. Writing daily, and accurately pointing to words while reading back one's writing, should help students understand and be able to apply this concept successfully. Other reading-based activities throughout the school day will assist with this as well, to the point that most students will not need more intensive instruction or special activities in order to consistently demonstrate the ability to space between words.

For those students who need it, continue to model and expect students to use their finger to space between words. Students should be encouraged to use finger spacing until their spacing is consistent and even. There will be students who consistently demonstrate spacing but place very large spaces between words. Asking them to use a finger again, and ensuring that they lay it down right next to the end of the previous word, will help show the perfect size for spaces between words.

A good strategy for students who are not spacing at all, or who do not space consistently, is the pattern strategy. Teach students that when they write they need to write a word, then put a finger space, write another word, then put a finger space. Shorten the prompt to *word, space, word, space*. If students are unsure exactly what words they are trying to write, help them formulate a sentence and then place their actual words into the pattern prompt. For example, "*The*, space, *dog*, space, *is*, space, *brown*."

There is another strategy to try, especially with those students who do not yet understand patterns. Draw a blank line for each word the student wants to write. Make sure the lengths of the lines correspond with the length of each word and leave spaces between the lines. Have the student write one or more sounds for each word on each line. The spaces between the lines will help emphasize the spaces that should be between words. If time allows, have the student rewrite the sentence, putting spaces in the exact same places where he or she sees them between the lines you drew. (This step did not occur in Gauge's sample shown at top right.)

Spacing is a reasonable goal for all kindergarten students who are capable of writing several words on the page. This does not, however, mean that all of your students will master this skill before they leave your class in May. But it is realistic to expect them to understand the purpose of and to at least try to use spaces.

You began modeling how and when to use finger spaces during the first six weeks of school. For some students, this will come quickly and naturally and will only need to be mentioned on a few rare occasions. Other students, even those who have a well-developed concept of words, may have difficulty figuring out where spaces go. Continue to teach them and expect them to use spaces between words. The effort required by you to develop this skill now, when students are just learning to write, will mitigate time spent on changing poor writing habits later. Eventually, where and when to use spaces will click for these students.

Additional ideas for teaching proper spacing can be found in the spacing section of Chapter 6, page 131.

Gauge, age 5 Creating write-on lines separated by even spaces can assist students in seeing what their thoughts look like.

Handwriting

To assist in improving not-yet-proficient handwriting, you will need to first carefully analyze a student's penmanship and presentation before individualizing instruction for improvement. Use the chart on the next page to check off the components of neat handwriting that students consistently demonstrate and to determine at which step to begin with the customized instruction. Be sure, with most learners anyway, that each previous step is in place before focusing your instruction on the next component.

Completing the chart will help you to know, during the delivery of individualized mini-lessons, which component of handwriting to focus on with each student. A thorough explanation of the sequential skills listed across the top of the chart can be found in Chapter 6 on pages 133–136. Remember also to prompt and expect students to use a correct pencil grasp so they will better be able to see the tips of their pencils as they write.

Junior, age 5 When you see that a student has not used proper spacing, do not ask him to erase the original writing and try it again with spaces. Erasing is hard work and uses up too much writing time. Instead, use the GLOW, GROW, SO formula and say, "You've got some good sounds, (GLOW) but your writing is hard to read without spaces in the right places." (GROW) "Don't erase it; let's just try to write it one more time down here with better spaces." (SO) The arrow indicates where the student should write and reminds him not to take the time to erase an entire sentence.

Handwriting Skills Record

Handwriting Skills

Students	1 Letters do not touch one another	2 Most letters are formed correctly and neatly (ongoing)	3 Mostly lowercase letters are used	4 Letters sit on real or perceived line	5 Tall letters are tall, short letters are short	6 Appropriate letters hang beneath the line	7 No reversals	8 Handwriting is nearly perfect

Students

Put a check under each handwriting skill that a student consistently demonstrates, beginning with 1. Focus individualized instruction on the first component not checked off.

Content and Fluency

According to the Kindergarten Writing Scoring Rubric, students must know what they are writing about and be able to read back their own writing with correct voice-print match to be considered proficient in the area of content and fluency. You may recall that this skill—being able to read back one's own writing—was really focused on and assessed during the months of October, November, December, and January. This means that the majority of your students will be able to accurately read back their own writing by spring and will therefore be proficient in this area. Intensifying instruction in this area will thus probably have more to do with fluency and getting students to write a greater number of sentences in one sitting.

Rarely do kindergartners lack motivation to write. Most of them are astounded by the whole notion of getting their pictures and ideas down on paper, especially when they discover that they and other people can read what they have written. If you assume that a student is not motivated to write because the student is not getting started once the topic has been given, it often may be that the student does not know enough about the topic or believe that he or she has anything worthwhile to say about it. In these instances, spend extra time with the student on your first trip around the room. Instead of just greeting him or her and writing the date on the journal page, have a brief conversation about the topic. Usually within a minute or two, the student will mention something that you find amusing, interesting, or just appropriate to write about. Your facial expressions and verbal reactions are crucial at this point. The student must truly believe that you think his or her idea is a great one and absolutely has to be written down.

Another reason students may not get started on or stick with their writing is they may sense they do not possess the skills necessary for getting their ideas on paper. With these students you will need to constantly repeat that the way to write is to listen to the sounds in the word and put down the ones that they know. That's it. The individualized mini-lesson might involve sitting beside the student and doing what used to be done with the whole class during the first six weeks of school:

- help the student formulate a short sentence; count the words in the sentence
- focus on the first word and decide if it is a word the student knows or a word for which he or she will need to listen to the sounds
- have the student write or copy the word from the word wall, or segment the sounds and have him or her choose just one for which he or she knows the letter
- repeat the process with the rest of the words until the student begins to see that his or her idea is appearing on the paper

Be wary of sitting with the student during this entire process for too many days in a row; this is independent writing time and you do not want him or her to become overly dependent upon you in order to write.

For some students, the main thing preventing them from getting more writing on their papers is their organization, pacing, and time-management skills. These are the students—there are usually one or two in a class—who get to school late, take longer than others to check their backpacks and get them hung up, need to talk to you about something before they are able to concentrate on their writing, need a tissue, cannot find pencils that work for them, or, once they are started, tend to take breaks between each letter they write on their paper. While it is appropriate initially to talk to these students about the importance of coming in and getting started quickly and to provide frequent reminders to stay on task and keep their pencils moving during writing time, the goal is for the students to be able to monitor themselves and make changes without continual prompts from you. To help students get started more quickly, it may be necessary to slowly count out loud to five, with students knowing that they must be in their seats and writing by the time you get to five. This can be done without disrupting the students who are already seated and engrossed in their writing. Any student who is still wandering about the classroom when you reach five will need to make up the writing time during recess. While the thought of supervising a student during recess time may sound like a punishment for you, doing it once or twice should be all it takes to get the student moving faster at the beginning of writing time. If missing a little recess time does not yield the desired results, then that consequence is not effective for that particular child and should not be continued anyway.

For the student who tends to sit and rest between each letter that is written, a tally mark system can be implemented. While circulating around the room, glance frequently at the student who tends to sit and do nothing. If he or she is working (as evidenced by moving the pencil on the paper, counting sounds on fingers, finding a letter in the alphabet, or checking the word wall for a spelling), then put a small tally mark in the corner of his or her journal page. After you have explained that tally marks are good and how to earn them, the student should be motivated to get as many as possible and will make a conscious effort to always be working. If the student understands how he or she earns tally marks, then all you need to do is try to catch the student in the act of writing and give him or her some positive feedback via the tally marks. This should not detract from your natural flow of movement about the room or the amount of attention the other students receive during writing time.

Another situation that sometimes arises is that a student may complete a sentence but does not have enough time to attempt another sentence. You might say, "You wrote a good sentence. Now I want you to write it one more time down here as fast as you can." The student will be able to write it much faster the second time, of course, because he or she needs only to copy the writing above rather than stopping to think through the sounds and letters to include. Writing it again will allow the student to physically experience more fluent writing and determine that he or she just might be capable of writing faster.

Whether it is motivation, skills, or time management that is interfering with a student's fluency, helping students realize what they can actually accomplish will be the most beneficial tactic for improvement. Just as a student may not realize that he or she knows how to spell certain words, the student also may not be cognizant of the fact that he or she is able to write one or more complete sentences and thus may not attempt to do so. Making this the focus of an individualized mini-lesson, or several consecutive mini-lessons, will help the student to see that indeed, he or she can do it.

You will find additional ideas for teaching content and fluency in Chapter 6, pages 136–138.

Sentence Structure

On the rubric, notice that students are expected to write one complete sentence by the end of kindergarten (the grade level goal is a score of 2 in that area). Most students will be able to write far more than this and their doing so will create more opportunities for mistakes in sentence structure.

When students read back their own writing, or when you read it back to them, they will usually be able to hear if a sentence is incomplete or if two ideas run together. They will not, however, always know what to do to fix the mistake. Encourage students to separate their ideas, to write just one of them at a time, and to constantly go back and reread what they are writing to make sure it is sounding the way they want it to. On the other end of the rubric, students who are able to write properly formed sentences on a consistent basis should be encouraged to try a variety of sentence beginnings and lengths. It is okay to point out that a student's sentences all start the exact same way and that the writing is a little boring to read because of it. Provide some examples for the student on how to say the same thing in a different way.

A few more teaching ideas can be found in the section on sentence structure in Chapter 6, pages 138–139.

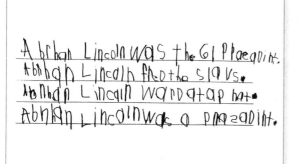

Anthony, age 6 Students will often use the same sentence beginning repeatedly because they have already gone through the process of listening to and separating the sounds and need now only copy for the latter sentences.

James, age 5 It is not uncommon for kindergarten students to borrow the last few words from one sentence and use them for the beginning of the next sentence. When they reread something like this, it often sounds okay to them. This is developmental and will correct itself on its own in due time. Therefore, it is not always necessary to point it out or have students try it again. When a student starts to recognize this as an error, then it will be appropriate to show him or her to fix it.

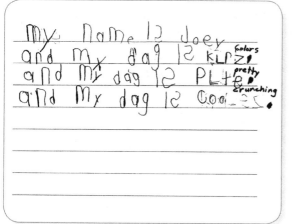

Joey, age 6 This student is using a monotonous pattern sentence structure because he is comfortable writing the sight words he knows but struggles when it comes to listening to sounds and recording letters for unknown words. Individualized mini-lessons with this student often focused on encouraging him to write more interesting sentences, even if it meant having to use words other than well-known sight words.

Periods as End Marks

Kindergarten students can and should learn that a period is used to indicate the end of an idea or to tell the reader to stop. Even if they know this and realize that writing contains periods, they will not necessarily start to experiment with them unless they are encouraged to do so. The scoring rubric indicates that students should have at least one period in their writing by the end of the school year, but that the period does not necessarily need to be in the correct place. Therefore, your main objective is to get students to try putting periods on their paper, anywhere, so that you can then start discussing where they should go.

For example, if a student tries to use a period but puts it in the wrong place, you can read his or her writing out loud and stop where indicated by the period. Then, ask the student if that sounds right and if he or she really wants you to stop there. The student will be able to hear as you read the writing aloud that the period is in the wrong place. Read the sentences again, stop where you should, and let the student put the period in the correct place.

If a student has only one sentence on his or her page and indicates that he or she is finished, support the child with a quick and effective prompt, embedded within a GLOW, GROW, SO format, such as, "Your sentence makes sense." (GLOW) "It *sounds* like you're done with your writing, but it doesn't *look* like you're done." (GROW) "How do you show you're finished?" (SO)

When a student has more than one idea written down, the most effective way to assist the student in determining where to put periods is to have the student read back his or her own writing and listen for when he or she pauses. If the student is unable to read fluently, then you should read the writing so he or she can listen for the breaks. Most students can hear the natural stopping points and correctly insert periods when prompted.

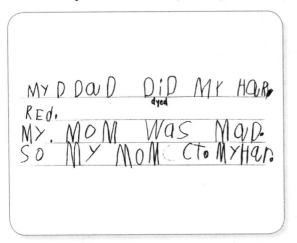

Norman, age 6 Now that this student has started experimenting with periods, it will be easier for a teacher to help him learn where they should go.

Once students get the gist of where periods go in their writing, and once the class is familiar with patterns, you can suggest a simple pattern to students to get them to capitalize the first word in their sentences. The pattern goes *period, capital, period, capital . . .* and reminds students that a period is always followed by a capital letter. Not many kindergarten students will master the use of end punctuation and capital letters at the beginning of sentences because they are so focused on their content and the incredible task analysis it takes to write the letters that make up their sentences. These conventions should be modeled, though, so that those students who are ready to try them have the opportunity to do so.

There are more ideas for teaching students about using periods in Chapter 6, on page 140.

IN REVIEW

The benefits of publishing, sharing, and celebrating student writing during these three months of the school year are limitless. You will see significant growth in your students' writing skills at a point in the year when you were probably already quite thrilled with what they were capable of doing. If, midyear, the acquisition of skills plateaus for some students, the prospect of their writing being turned into a book should generate new enthusiasm and motivation to write more or write even better than before. Also, publicizing students' writing will intensify their passion for writing. When students begin to understand that their writing can be read and enjoyed by others, just like the writing of actual authors of real books, their appreciation for the act of writing and their pride in their abilities and creativity will be obvious and contagious. Last, but not least, the repeated reading and sharing of these student books will dramatically affect students' reading skills and how they see themselves as readers. Though publishing student writing and letting students illustrate and share their work takes time, it is time well spent. There is no other instructional activity that will generate such marked increases in passion and skill level.

Chapter Five

Writing Projects to Finish the Year: May

During this busy, transitional month, students apply their writing skills to a variety of writing topics and projects designed to spark their interests and maintain their proficiencies. Writing instruction involves selecting appropriate and motivating projects for students to work and continue to learn, right up until the last day of school.

DAILY WRITING TIME

May is a difficult month for teaching because students, even kindergartners, can sense that things are winding down and that a transition is approaching. The process of publishing books in the previous three months served as a great motivator and the result was a sudden and rapid increase in writing skills, stamina, and fluency. While students may lose a little ground after the period of publishing comes to a halt, the writing they embark upon in this last month can help them practice key skills and keep them motivated to write. Maintaining this rigor through to the last day of school will also help limit the skills regression over the summer.

Once the three-month period ends, it will not be very effective to expect students to just go back to the usual writing about a daily provided topic. Your students will have already learned, at this tender young age, that writing should be purposeful.

Following are end-of-year ideas that have worked well for my students and for me.

- **Curriculum-Based Topics**

    Often in April and May, teachers take a quick peek at the curriculum to ensure they have indeed covered everything that is included for their grade level. Scanning the various subject areas in the curriculum may provide some ideas for writing, whether writing about them would be a venue for teaching them or, if you have already addressed them, a way of reviewing the subject matter. For curriculum topics that were covered earlier in the year when students' writing skills were limited, reviewing them might be worthwhile because the students are now more able to write about them meaningfully. For example, if the class discussed when to call 911 at the beginning of the school year, perhaps students could now write scenarios in which calling 911 would be appropriate. To review patterns, students might draw patterns in their journals and then write the words to describe the patterns. With science concepts, such as living and nonliving things, students might choose something they believe fits the description of living and write about the characteristics that lead them to believe that it is or was alive. Glancing again at the curriculum will generate some ideas for purposeful writing during the month of May.

- **Letter Writing**

    Letter writing is a perfect activity for this time of year. Students are quite capable by now of writing a quality letter. There are many people to whom your students can write, and because someone will be reading them and possibly replying, the students' desire for an audience for their writing will be fulfilled. The first person to whom each student should write a letter is next year's first-grade teacher. That students do not yet know who their teachers are going to be does not matter. The letters can be addressed as, "To My 1st Grade Teacher," or simply, "Dear Teacher." The purpose for having students write letters is not to have an opportunity to teach the correct format of letter writing (unless that is included in the kindergarten curriculum), but for the students to have a meaningful reason to write.

    Rather than just announce one day that the writing topic is a letter to next year's teacher, do some preliminary teaching on the concept of a letter and what one might include in a letter. Generally, kindergarten students at this point in the year can understand and apply the expectation that their letters be at least three sentences long. The first sentence should be a greeting and/or an introduction of oneself. An example that most kindergarten students can write is, "Hi! My name is _____." The second sentence can tell something the

Nicole, age 6 Letters to the first-grade teacher reveal students' hopes and personalities, as well as showcase their writing skills.

student really liked about kindergarten and the third can be an inquiry about first grade or can tell what the student is hoping for in first grade.

If letters are to be written during daily journal writing time, then students should be encouraged to spend more than one day on the letter if additional time is needed. Also, students may surely write more than three sentences if they so desire. The letter to next year's teacher should be kept and delivered once it is determined who the teacher is. It then serves as both an introduction to the child, as well as a writing sample, composed when that student's writing skills were at their peak.

Students can also write letters to the various people who have taught them or have been a part of their lives during kindergarten, including the specialist teachers (physical education, music, library, and so forth), volunteers, instructional aides, the principal, custodians, bus drivers, lunchroom personnel, and favorite substitute teachers. The best part about having students write letters is that they may receive replies back from those to whom letters have been sent. This will be quite rewarding and uplifting for those students suffering from the post-publishing blues.

List Writing

Another fun and new writing activity for the month of May is list writing. Writing a list differs from the typical writing that students have been doing in that the students will use a single word or short phrase for each idea they write rather than a complete sentence. Just as with letter writing, model the writing of a list before asking students to write one.

An easy type of list for kindergarten students to start with is a list of favorites. They can list their favorite foods, favorite games, favorite television programs, favorite places, or titles of favorite books. When modeling how to write a list, compare and contrast a true list format (containing single words or short phrases numbered down the paper), with something written in an incorrect format. The incorrect list should show complete sentences, with repetitive portions, numbered but going straight across the paper (e.g., *1. My favorite food is pizza. 2. My favorite food is ice cream. 3. My favorite food is salad.*), since this is the most common error that kindergarten students will make if they do not immediately understand the format of a list. Students should try other types of lists as well. They can once again review the various curriculum areas by writing lists as a way to demonstrate what they know. Examples include writing lists of appropriate clothing for the four different seasons, listing healthy food items, or creating a list of things they know about the different coins.

Descriptions

By May, kindergarten students are capable of learning how to write descriptions and this can serve as a basis for some out-of-the-ordinary journal writing. Again, since this is something new, model what it means to describe something. Students often enjoy describing characters they have met in shared reading and read-aloud stories, such as *The Gingerbread Man* and

Johnny Appleseed. Once students get accustomed to including the most salient features of a character in their descriptions, you can start a guessing game where the class tries to guess whom the student is describing. Other topics that can be described include bedrooms, the playground, the daily schedule, special class activities, field trips, and interesting places the students have been.

Providing students with something concrete and tangible to describe is also stimulating. You might set out a bag of plastic bugs, a pile of buttons, or a sampling of small treats. As students come into the classroom they can choose one item, take it with them to their seats, and begin writing about whatever it is they chose, either describing the item or using it as a basis for a story or some information writing. The month of May is a time to get creative and a little experimental with your writing topics for your students, with the primary goal being to maintain students' skills and eagerness for writing.

SKILLS ASSESSMENT: COMPILING DATA

If you previously assessed letter names, letter sounds, the stage of spelling development, and/or how many points students earned for each skill on the writing scoring rubric, then it would be beneficial to repeat these assessments midyear as well as at the end of the school year. Administering the same assessments in the spring that you administered in the fall or midyear is typically quite rewarding because the comparison provides concrete evidence that the majority of students are responding to your instruction. Individual student improvement, as well as classwide gains, can be easily documented.

Take the time to analyze the end-of-the-year assessment data you collect to determine the amount and type of growth shown by each student. This is more readily done by preparing charts or lists that show the various assessment scores in ascending or descending order and the percentage of students you consider having met or surpassed the expected score. Prepare for parents a copy of each chart with all of the student names deleted except their child's so the information can be distributed without jeopardizing student confidentiality. Once again, having the assessment results of the entire class will give parents the opportunity to draw conclusions about their child's scores in comparison to his or her earlier scores, to curricular expectations, and to other students. If you are pleased with the results shown on the charts, by all means share them with the principal so he or she also will be fully apprised of what has transpired in your classroom this school year.

More important than individual student scores is looking at the results of the class as a whole in order to evaluate the effectiveness of your writing instruction. What percentage of students learned all or nearly all of the letter names and letter sounds? How many of them can confidently and accurately segment words into individual sounds? Have 100 percent of students reached at least the partially phonetic stage of spelling development? Is a very large percentage beyond the expected partially phonetic stage and well into the phonetic (and possibly even transitional) stage of spelling? With what knowledge did the students begin school? How effectively are students applying their knowledge base to the process of writing? What percentage of students are proficient (score of at least 2 points in each of the six subskills) on the Kindergarten Writing Scoring Rubric? What information can be obtained from any additional assessments you used? These are the questions we must ask and answer to determine what we can improve in next year's daily writing instruction.

As I have strengthened my approach, I've been able to get the kind of results that exceed expectations and help students lay the foundation for impressive literacy growth. Every year, more than 90 percent of my students are able to do the following by May:

- learn all the letter names and all the consonant sounds as well as several of the various sounds for vowels
- reach the phonetic stage of spelling development or beyond and apply common letter chunks and word endings in their writing
- read and spell a greater-than-expected number of sight words
- quickly and easily write several related sentences

These results were obtained in half-day and full-day kindergarten programs, with several students arriving each year with no knowledge of letter names or sounds and limited exposure to writing, books, or text. Results like this are possible, and with structured daily writing, should be expected in kindergarten classrooms across the nation.

IN REVIEW

While you will be teaching right up to the last day of school, keep in mind that May is also a time to reflect and to let go. Know that you have given your students that which they most needed from you—the opportunity to write every single day of the school year and the expectation and support necessary to write up to their potential each and every one of those times. You brought them as far as you possibly could have in the area of writing. Some students are not quite where you hoped they would be by this time; others have far exceeded what you ever imagined possible for kindergarten students. It is now time to let them go, time to entrust them to their next teachers, time to know that there is no better start these students could have had for a lifelong love of writing.

Students	Sight Words	Reading Level			Stage of Spelling	Writing Sample	
	from a list of 100	Level	Accuracy	Retell	Scored with Kdgn. Scoring Rubric	Scoring Rubric	
						1st	2nd
Points Possible →	from a list of 100			3		24	
Target Score →	20	3/C	93%	2	partially phonetic	12	
Student #1	20	2/B – mid kdgn.	100%	3	partially phonetic	15	14
Student #2	64	12/G – March 1st grade	96%	2	phonetic/transitional	21	18
Student #3 (ELL)	61	12/G – March 1st grade	95%	2	phonetic	20	20
Student #4	99	34/O – mid 3rd grade	94%	2	phonetic	22	22
Student #5	83	16/I – end of 1st grade	94%	3	phonetic	22	22
Student #6	77	12/G – March 1st grade	98%	2	phonetic	17	NA
Student #7	100	34/O – mid 3rd grade	97%	2	transitional	24	24
Student #8 (IEP)	NA	NA (nonverbal student)	NA	NA	random	NA	NA
Student #9 (IEP)	69	12/G – March 1st grade	96%	2	phonetic	15	16
Student #10	28	6/D – Nov. 1st grade	94%	3	partially phonetic	18	17
Student #11	99	28/M – end of 2nd grade	95%	3	transitional	21	22
Student #12	45	4/C – begin. 1st grade	94%	3	partially phonetic	13	15
Student #13	51	4/C – begin. 1st grade	97%	3	phonetic	19	19
Student #14	77	12/G – March 1st grade	96%	3	phonetic	15	18
Student #15	33	3/C – end of kdgn.	98%	3	phonetic	NA	22
Student #16 (ELL)	95	18/J – begin. 2nd grade	95%	3	phonetic	22	15
Student #17	74	16/I – end of 1st grade	94%	3	phonetic	16	15
Student #18	88	18/J – begin. 2nd grade	97%	3	phonetic	22	22
Student #19	95	24/L – mid 2nd grade	97%	2	phonetic	12	22
Student #20	94	30/N – begin. 3rd grade	95%	3	phonetic	23	NA
Average Not including student #8	71					18.7	19
% Meeting Target Not including student #8	100%	95%	—	—	100%	100%	100%

*This chart shows the end-of-year assessment results from a full-day/every-day kindergarten class that participated in this approach to daily writing. The expectation to correctly spell high-frequency words and common letter chunks had a huge impact on students' writing ability and their reading levels. Notice that the students' knowledge of letter names and sounds is not recorded here; when skills are this advanced, it is understood that most of these students know not only the letter names and sounds but also the sounds letters make when combined with various other letters.

Chapter Six

More Strategies, Tips, and Mini-Lessons for Independent Writing

The intent of this chapter is to share a variety of student writing samples and discuss the teaching opportunities each one affords. I provide instructional ideas, skills to target, and examples of age-appropriate language to use with kindergartners, along with mini-lessons that I've actually conducted with the student writers. With some of the writing samples, it may seem that there are more timely or obvious teaching points than the one I chose for the individualized mini-lesson. This is most likely due to the fact that the student's abilities, current needs, and history of interactions with the teacher cannot be portrayed in the single writing sample shown. When possible and necessary, I've filled in background information that serves as an explanation for the direction I took with the student.

The writing samples and individualized mini-lessons included have been divided into seven main categories, six of which appear on the Kindergarten Writing Scoring Rubric (page 92):

- Routines and procedures
- Sound-letter correspondence
- Spacing
- Handwriting
- Content and fluency
- Sentence structure
- Periods as end marks

SELECTING SKILLS TO TEACH DURING INDIVIDUALIZED MINI-LESSONS

A typical student's writing will develop in all six areas on the Kindergarten Writing Scoring Rubric simultaneously, although some skills may stretch out to the right of the rubric faster than others. Keep these skills and the order in which they appear on the rubric in mind as you deliver individualized mini-lessons; doing so will help you decide what your focus should be for each student. The GLOW, GROW, SO formula described in Chapter 3 is used as a basis, in one format or another, for most of the individualized mini-lessons that follow. Keep in mind that the purpose of individualized mini-lessons is not to help students revise and edit their writing until all mistakes have been corrected, but to focus on one or two elements of writing that a student can immediately improve upon and learn from.

Routines and Procedures

Sometimes mini-lessons must focus on helping students with procedural skills that ensure they use their time efficiently and effectively and set themselves up for success.

Starting at the Top

Tip: In both reading and writing instruction at the beginning of the year, introduce the phrase *down and back* (or something similar) when you model return sweeps. Continue to use the cue you've chosen consistently.

Dylan's Mini-Lesson: "You wrote so much today that you had to start another line of writing." (GLOW) "What are we supposed to do if we write all the way across the paper, get to the edge, and run out of room? We're supposed to go down and back. It looks like you went *up* and back. Do you know why you did that? It's because you didn't have any more room at the bottom of your paper. So you couldn't go down." (GROW) "One of the reasons we start writing at the top of our paper instead of way down here at the bottom is so that we will always have room to go down and back. Tomorrow, I want you to be sure to start writing at the *top* of your paper. And if you write a whole bunch again, like you did today, then you'll be able to try going down and back." (SO)

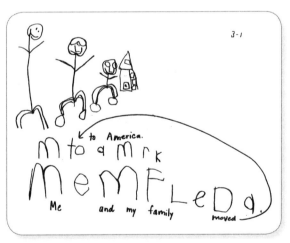

Dylan, age 6 This student could not execute a return sweep correctly because he started writing too closely to the bottom of the paper.

Dan, age 5 Dan's drawing is so big that it took up most of the space on his paper, forcing him to write his letters down the left side of the paper.

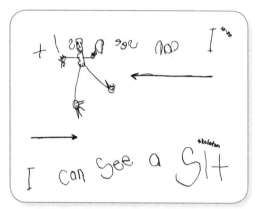

Grant, age 5 Grant is able to reverse his writing so it reads right to left.

Madi, age 5 When Madi erased her sentence and then rewrote it, with spaces, over her original try, I had her write the sentence a third time, with spaces between the words and in a clean area on the paper. Notice that she tried to erase the upper sentence yet again and that she changed *apo* to *apple* after seeing my underwriting, both indicators that she wants her work to look perfect.

Drawing at the Bottom

Tip: It is especially important when students use unlined paper to monitor where they are beginning their drawings. Drawings can easily fill the writing space and limit or crowd what students are able to write.

Dan's Mini-Lesson: "I like your flag." (GLOW) "It's so big, though. You hardly had room to write any letters, and you had to write them going down instead of across." (GROW) "Let's see if we can squeeze some words in right here on this stripe. I'll help you listen to the sounds." After we've finished, I say, "Tomorrow I want to see you draw a small picture at the bottom of the paper and leave room to write *across* the paper, okay?" (SO)

Writing Across the Paper From Left to Right

Tip: It is not uncommon for kindergartners to unexpectedly write something backwards; and, fascinatingly, when they do, it will almost always be a perfect mirror image. If this happens on only a few random instances, do not worry; just gently remind the student about the direction in which we write.

Grant's Mini-Lesson: "I can see that you wrote about a skeleton, (GLOW) but it is kind of hard to read because you wrote in the wrong direction." (GROW) "Can you show me where we start on the paper? And which way do we always go? Remember, you can look at the ONE WAY sign if you can't remember which direction to go. Why don't you write your sentence one more time down here going the right way?" (SO)

Learning When to Erase

Madi's Mini-Lesson: "Oh good, I see spaces between your words now, (GLOW) but I still can't read what you wrote because it's so dark from all that erasing. (GROW) "Remember, I don't want you spending so much time erasing. Now, I still want to see if you can write your idea with spaces between your words, but in a clean place on your paper." (SO)

Because erasing was the obvious teaching point with Madi on this day, I did not bring up the fact that she changed her writing and copied my underwriting. Had the circumstances been different, it would have been prudent to remind her that I need to see her writing and the way she spells words and that changing it and copying me is not allowed, unless I specifically ask her to do so.

Trying Again With a Practice Box

Tip: Practice boxes are effective tools for individualized mini-lessons. First, they provide a well-defined area in which the student can attempt what you have asked. This reminds students that you do not want them to erase their original writing. In addition, practice boxes will immediately catch your eye as you circulate back to students, reminding you to give feedback on that specific word.

Ha's Mini-Lesson: "I can read this, (GLOW) but I see two words that don't quite have the right sounds." (GROW) "Show me the sounds for *need* on your fingers. . . . Now show me the sounds for *phone* on your fingers. . . . Good. Will you please put the right sounds for *need* and *phone* in these practice boxes?" (SO) Most students will need to count and record the sounds for one word at a time, but this particular student could handle talking about both words with me and then writing them by himself.

Spelling Word Wall Words Correctly: Fix-Up Circles

Tip: If a student incorrectly writes a word that has been formally introduced to the class and added to the word wall then you should circle it. Students soon learn that when you circle a word it is an indication that they "know" the word and that you expect them to find the correct spelling, either in their minds or somewhere in the classroom, and to fix the spelling by erasing what is there and writing it correctly. Most students will be able to do this independently, allowing you to move on and return later for closure. Compare fix-up circles to practice boxes and point out to students that with fix-up circles, it is okay to erase and correct a mistake; with practice boxes, students should leave their first attempt and try again in a different spot. Fix-up circles are effective tools for individualized mini-lessons; like practice boxes, they will instantly get your attention as you circulate back to the student, reminding you that feedback is needed on that word.

Sound-Letter Correspondence

The majority of your individualized mini-lessons will focus on supporting students in their development of more sophisticated spelling. An explanation of the stages of spelling development is provided on pages 89–91.

Moving Into Stage 2: Partially Phonetic Spelling

This is an exciting phase, in which students move from random-letter spelling to using letters to represent sounds, as shown in Dana's sample from October.

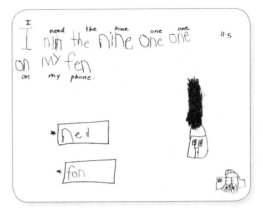

Ha, age 5 This sample shows the use of practice boxes for spelling with sound segmentation.

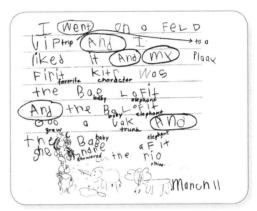

Hannah, age 6 Although her misspellings are corrected, Hannah initially spelled *went* and *and* incorrectly. Since these words were on the class word wall and Hannah had written *and* several times in her piece, I circled the words and asked her to spell them correctly. Though the correct spelling of sight words seemed most pressing, future lessons might focus on avoiding repetition and using lowercase *a*'s to spell *and*.

Dana, age 5 To help this student progress into the partially phonetic stage of spelling, I asked that she write at least the word *a* or *the* (she already knew both of these words or could find them on the word wall) and at least one sound that represents the picture she drew. Read more about this two-word combination technique in Chapter 7, page 158.

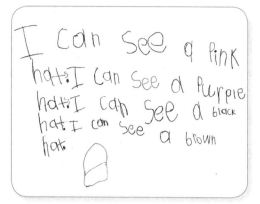

Charissa, age 5 This student wrote all known words and color words, which she copied from the color chart. She did not risk writing any words that she needed to sound out.

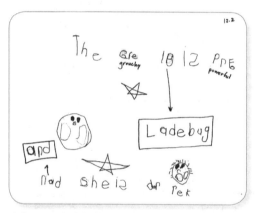

Jake, age 6 Jake has been in the partially phonetic stage of spelling development for several months and needs a little push to include more sounds in his writing.

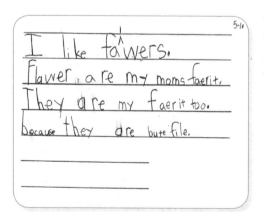

Angie, age 5 Angie, knowing she should not do a lot of erasing, decided to use a caret to amend her mistake.

Using Two Types of Words

Tip: Remember, students should be encouraged to write both known words and words that require listening to the sounds. You can elicit different word choices from a student by asking him or her to respond to certain questions about what he or she has already written. Asking why, when, or where often works well.

Charissa's Mini-Lesson: "I can see that you're pretty good at using the color chart." (GLOW) "Can you tell me something about the hat besides what color it is, like where you got the hat or why you have a hat?" (GROW) "These would be good things to write instead of just telling me about different hat colors." (SO)

Moving Into Stage 3: Phonetic Spelling

Jake's Mini-Lesson: "It looks like you wrote a sentence about the grouchy ladybug." (GLOW) "What about the word *ladybug*? *Lll-aaa-d-eee-b-uuu-g*. It seems like a pretty long word that has more than two sounds." (GROW) "Try *ladybug* in this practice box. See how many sounds you can hear and write down." (SO)

Recording Sounds That Are Heard

Tip: The beginning sound of a word is not always the most easily heard sound. For example, beginning writers may represent *leaf* with *e*, because they hear the /e/ sound most prominently. When students are first learning to record letters for the sounds they hear, encourage them to write down any sound they can isolate and/or know the letter for.

Blending Sounds

Angie's Mini-Lesson: "I see you wrote about flowers today." (GLOW) "Now, the first time you wrote *flowers*, you started with a plain /f/ sound. The next time you used a /fl/ blend. Which one do you think is the best?" (GROW) Angie responded by making a caret and the letter *l*. "Wow! You decided to use a caret to fix that word. Good job!" (SO and GLOW)

Correctly Sequencing Sounds

Brittany's Mini-Lesson: "What a nice neat sentence." (GLOW) "Let's see if I can read it. *I can see a pink a-h-t.*" Brittany looked at me quizzically, as if I accidentally misread what she wrote. "That's what you wrote. What did you want this sentence to say?" (GROW) As Brittany told me, she began to figure out her mistake. I asked Brittany to separate and count out the sounds in *hat* on her fingers and then try to write the sounds in the correct order on the lines provided. (SO)

Supporting Students with Articulation Needs

Tip: It is not always easy to know what you can expect from students who have difficulty articulating some sounds. The best course of action is to consult a speech and language specialist for guidance.

Craig's Mini-Lesson: The speech and language specialist told me that Craig should be able to represent /*th*/ in his writing. If he weren't able to do so, I would have him refer to the word wall to find words with this challenging sound. "You did a nice job of listening to the sounds and writing down what you heard." (GLOW) "You really have to think about some of these words when you're writing. I'm getting confused by these words you wrote: *dayer* and *din*." (GROW) "Listen to the way I say *there* and watch my mouth. Do you see my tongue sticking out? See if you can write down the right beginning sound." I repeat the "SO" instruction for *then*. (SO)

Moving Into Stage 4: Transitional Spelling

Tip: I teach three common word endings to kindergartners: *-s*, *-ing*, and *-ed*. I remind students that the *-ed* ending sometimes makes a /*t*/ sound. A great reminding rhyme for this is, "It sounds like a *t*, but it's really *-ed*."

Alec's Mini-Lesson: "Wow! You wrote a lot today about our show on the stage. Can you read it to me?" (GLOW) Alec reads the last sentence *I like it* as "I liked it." "If you want it to say *I liked it* at the end, you'll have to change *like* into *liked*. We've learned how to do that. Do you remember?" (GROW) Alec isn't sure how to proceed. "Remember, there are three endings we can stick on the end of words. What are they? Yes, *-s* is one of them. And *-ed*. And *-ing*. I'll write those here and then you choose the one you think will change *like* into *liked*." (SO)

Brittany, age 6

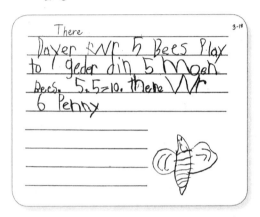

Craig, age 5 Notice the student wrote *dayer* for *there*, *togeder* for *together*, and *din* for *then*. I prepared these questions for the speech and language specialist. Is Craig able to produce the /*th*/ sound if he really thinks about it first? Even if he cannot produce it, does he realize that other people do not say *togeder*? Since he knows the word *the*, should I expect him to make a connection between that word and *there* and *then* and figure out that the latter two start with the same sound as *the*?

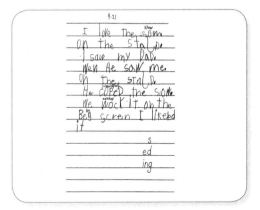

Alec, age 6 Alec read his writing to me using the past tense, but forgot to use the *-ed* ending in his writing. Providing ending choices helped him revise the verb tense in the last line.

Spacing

Spacing between words should develop along with students' ability to use sound-letter correspondence.

Understanding the Concept of Word

Tip: When you see writing like Sarah's, at right, one way to encourage the use of spaces is to draw a line for each word the student has written toward the bottom of the paper or wherever there is room. Lay your finger down between the lines as you draw them to make it obvious that there are indeed spaces between the words. Most students who do not space between words will be unable to write one word per line on their own, so this is typically a mini-lesson where you will need to pull up a chair and stay with the student while he or she attempts this. Notice that when I provided a separate line for each word, Sarah was able to hear and record more than just one sound for most of the words.

Learning That Spacing Allows Others to Read Our Writing

T.J.'s Mini-Lesson: "It looks like you wrote something about a man." (GLOW) "Can you read it to me?" After T.J. reads, I say, "Do you know why you had to read it to me instead of me just reading it by myself? It's because there aren't any spaces between your words. The only word I could read was *man* because it has spaces on both sides and I can see it here all by itself." (GROW) "Try your sentence one more time down here with finger spaces." (SO)

Using the Pattern Strategy for Spacing

Tip: Use an arrow to show students where to try again and to subtly remind them that they should not erase.

Davis's Mini-Lesson: "It looks like you've got a good idea going here. Can you read it to me?" (GLOW) Davis reads the sentence. "Oh, thanks. I was having a little trouble reading it because there aren't any spaces. Remember that pattern I taught you? When we write we have to write a word, do a finger space, write a word, do a finger space." (GROW) "Let's try that together." (SO)

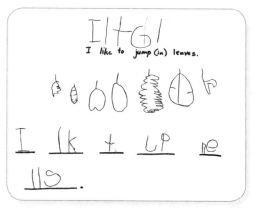

Sarah, age 5 Sarah demonstrates classic beginning sound writing, which indicates that she probably understands the concept of words and is ready to start spacing between words.

T.J., age 5 This student's writing reveals a clear message when I help him write with spaces.

Davis, age 5 This student is still struggling, in April, with adding spacing between words. I take an approach that reminds him to follow a pattern, since he's good with patterns.

Handwriting

Students generally acquire the following eight skills for precise handwriting *sequentially*. Familiarize yourself with them, use the chart on page 114 to track students who struggle, and keep all this in mind as you deliver individualized mini-lessons.

1. Letters Do Not Touch One Another

Tip: Teach students that each letter they write gets its own space. It cannot touch any other letter. Most students will pick up on this important concept of handwriting during the initial six weeks of modeled writing and will not need much instruction regarding it. Occasionally, a student will write a letter that ends up touching the previous letter; if so, the student should erase it right away and scoot it over. If a student has many letters that touch one another, have the student practice rewriting one group of letters, trying extra hard not to let them touch each other. The student may need reminders to slow down and try to control the pencil. Before long, the student should realize that he or she is capable of doing this and that it is easier to write carefully the first time than to go back and erase.

2. Letter Formation

Tips: You will need to explicitly teach the proper formation of letters (see letter formation cues on pages 43–45) both during and outside of journal writing time from the very beginning of kindergarten and continually support students' letter formation practice throughout the year. The key aspect is that students be supervised when focusing on and practicing letter formation. You or a supervising adult will need to notice mistakes in formation, point them out to the student, and help him or her try again immediately. Otherwise, letter formation will not develop properly or improve. See pages 151–155 in Chapter 7 for ideas on how best to implement handwriting practice in your classroom.

While you are circulating during journal writing time and delivering individualized mini-lessons, reiterate to students that most letters are formed by starting at the top and not lifting the pencil unless absolutely necessary. Insist, too, that students form letters neatly, not just correctly. For example, if students circle backward to make an *o*, as they should, they should also take care to close the *o* in the exact same spot as they started it, so it ends up looking like a perfect circle. Letter formation differs from the other steps that should be taken to improve a child's handwriting in that it is ongoing and does not need to be mastered before moving on to step three. Most students will need the entire school year to master the proper formation of all the letters.

Katrina's Mini-Lesson: "We've been working on the way you write your letters, right? I see that you made some of your lowercase *m*'s correctly," (GLOW) "but that others have points or no sticks on them." (GROW) "I'm going to put some lines down here at the bottom and I want you to practice some lowercase *m*'s. Put one *m* on each line. When you write them, be sure to say, 'go down, trace it up, bump, bump' and they'll probably end up looking the way they're supposed to. Good luck! I'll be back to check them." (SO) I stay and watch Katrina write the first *m*, reminding her to say the cue as she writes the letter.

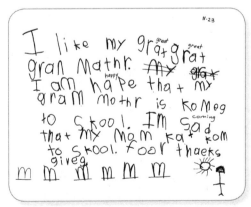

Katrina, age 5 A quick glance at Katrina's writing indicates that her handwriting is the skill that needs the most attention. She is already above proficiency in the other areas of sound-letter correspondence, spacing, content and fluency, sentence structure, and periods as end marks.

3. Lowercase Letters

Tip: Students should use mostly lowercase letters in their writing. If they are writing primarily capital letters, then have them rewrite words or complete sentences in lowercase letters until they are familiar with the way the majority of the letters look. Encourage students to look at the classroom alphabet or their journal covers for the correct formations. Having mostly lowercase letters for models on the journal cover page and around the room indirectly encourages students to use these letters as opposed to capitals.

Kay's Mini-Lesson: "Your handwriting is very neat and that makes it easy for me to read what you wrote." (GLOW) "Don't forget, though, that you

Kay, age 5 One of the first steps in helping a student write more conventionally is to make sure she is using mostly lowercase letters.

need to use almost all lowercase letters when you write. The only letter that should be a capital is the very first letter you wrote." (GROW) "So, I want you to write this exact same sentence one more time with mostly lowercase letters. If you need to, look at the alphabet to see how the lowercase letters should look." (SO)

4. Set Letters on the Line

Tip: Setting letters on a real or perceived line is a precursor to comparing the height of letters. If students are working on unlined paper and it is obvious they are having difficulty picturing where the line would be, draw it in for them so they can better see that some of their letters are not sitting on the line. Sometimes I refer to the line as the *ground* and to letters that are off the ground as *floating away* or as *floaters.* During journal time, have these students rewrite one or two words until they have set all the letters on the line. Do not focus, at this point, on letters that hang below the line; if students hang them below, great, but if they are not yet doing this then it is appropriate to allow them to form the letters so they too sit on the ground line for now.

Clerissa, age 5 This student shows proficiency with the first three skills of handwriting and is ready to practice setting all letters on the line.

Clerissa's Mini-Lesson: "I like how almost all of your letters are lowercase and written neatly. You seem like the type of kid who wants to have really nice handwriting." (GLOW) "If you want your writing to be even better, make sure every single letter you write touches the ground line. All letters that we write should touch the ground line—tall letters, short letters, and even letters that hang down." (GROW) "Can you point to three letters you think are floating away? Good. Change those three letters so they touch the line, and then tomorrow try to have all your letters touch the line." (SO)

5. Tall Letters and Short Letters

Tall Letters: *all capital letters, b, d, f, h, k, l, t*

Short Letters: *a, c, e, g, i, j, m, n, o, p, q, r, s, u, v, w, x, y, z*

Tip: If students are not already doing so, they should start making tall letters taller and/or short letters shorter until there is a clear distinction between the two. It is usually not necessary to provide a top line and a bottom line in order for students to make letter heights distinguishable in their writing, but it may be helpful for some students. (A dotted middle line is not necessary and will usually complicate matters at this point.) Facilitate attending to letter height by having students rewrite individual letters or entire words with the correct letter height. Most students will soon begin thinking about and incorporating this into their writing with fewer and fewer prompts from you.

Notice that *g, j, p, q,* and *y* are placed in the short letter category. They are, of course, hang-down letters, but students have to learn that even though they hang down, they cannot start "way up high." Additionally, students may notice that lowercase *t* is not as tall as the other tall letters. When they are ready, you can begin to remind students of *t*'s slightly lower height by referring to it as *teenager t* and to the other tall letters as grown-ups.

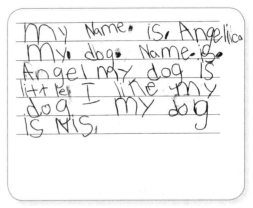

Angelica, age 5 Note that although Angelica's letters are formed correctly they are almost all the same height. To remedy this, I focus Angelica's attention on letter height and encourage her to write short letters smaller.

6. Hang-Down Letters

Hang-Down Letters: *g, j, p, q, y*

Tip: Often students will be hesitant to hang letters beneath the line because the letters might end up interfering with the writing that will be on the line below. Let them know that it is okay in this situation for a letter to touch another letter. Next, be sure students can discriminate which letters actually hang down lower than the others. Have them show these letters to you on their journal cover or in another alphabet. Once they know which letters hang down, expect students to put forth some effort on getting them to hang below the line. Choose one or two from their writing each day for students to practice.

Tanner's Mini-Lesson: "When I look at your writing I don't see very many things that need to be fixed." (GLOW) "But I do notice one thing. The letters that are supposed to hang down aren't hanging down at all. Instead, they look like tall letters." (GROW) "Can you find the letters in your writing that should be hanging down below the ground line? Will you work on changing those for me so they look right the next time I come around?" (SO)

Tanner, age 5 Notice the lowercase *y*'s, *g*'s, and *p*'s in Tanner's writing. They are formed correctly, but they do not hang below the line as they should.

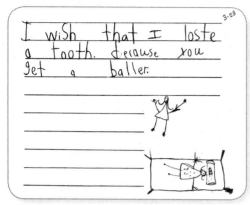

Noelle, age 6

7. Reversals

Tip: Students are usually able to perceive that a letter is written backwards once it has been pointed out to them. They often will not notice on their own, however. Initially, just choose one letter from a student's writing that is reversed and ask her to write the word again, in a practice box, with all letters going the right direction. Soon you can say, "I see a backwards letter in this word. Do you see it?" Once you have determined which letter(s) students consistently reverse, make them aware of this information and then expect them to be proactive by predicting that they may write certain letters backwards, and if they do, to erase them and write them correctly without you mentioning it.

It is helpful to have these students find one word with their particular troublesome letter in it that they really know how to write well and with which they never reverse that letter. Then have them picture that word in their mind or find the word in the classroom while writing the problematic letter so there is a better chance they will write it in the correct direction. Also, remind students of the letter formation cues and, if the act of saying a cue while writing the letter will prevent a reversal, ask them to say the cue every time they write the letter. Eventually, hold students completely accountable for noticing and fixing reversals on their own by saying, "Remember, it's *your* responsibility to figure out what direction that letter should be going."

Noelle's Mini-Lesson: "I see some erasing around this *d* and this *b*, and that tells me you were really thinking about which direction these letters should go. I'm glad you were thinking about it." (GLOW) "It didn't turn out the right way though. Did you know that?" (GROW) "Don't forget that it's your responsibility to make sure they look right. If you can't remember in your mind how to make them, all you have to do is look around the room and find a *b* or a *d* to copy. And don't forget that lowercase *d* starts with a *c*; that will make your *d* turn out right on the word *dollar*." (SO)

8. Nearly Perfect Handwriting

Students who make it this far through all the handwriting improvement steps usually don't need further guidance with forming letters more precisely. Sometimes, however, students will master all seven components listed above, but their handwriting still will not look quite right. And often it can be difficult to determine exactly what is keeping it from looking as good as possible. If there is anything in a student's handwriting that can still be improved upon, it is probably letter formation. Try tracing over some of a student's writing, starting at the exact same places the student did, forming your letters exactly as he or she did. By doing this, you will see exactly which letters were formed incorrectly. To perfect the student's letter formation, review the proper formation of these letters and then expect the student to form more and more of them correctly as time goes on.

Content and Fluency

One of the most delightful features of kindergarten writing is the content. Anyone fortunate enough to spend their days with this age group knows these youngsters say many amusing and insightful things. These thoughts will gradually appear in their writing once their fluency is developed to a point where they can get more than a few words down on paper. Avoid squelching their unique voices by trying to alter or improve their content. Students will have plenty of guidance in content, structure, and organization of ideas in the next several years of school when they are better able to understand this instruction.

Another aspect of content is fluency. Fluency refers to a student's ability to get meaningful and readable sentences down on paper in a timely fashion. If students do not write more than one sentence during a 25- to 30-minute block of writing time, then they will not get as much practice writing as some of the other students, and it will not be as easy to find teaching points and provide instruction to them. Also, the more students write, the more students will read; increasing a student's volume of writing will directly impact the student's overall growth in literacy.

Physical and mental stamina play a part in students' ability to get words down on paper or to write for the full writing period. To develop this stamina, encourage students to write a little bit more, or a little bit faster, each day. Also, be sure to explicitly state your expectation that students work during the entire journal writing time. If a student is just sitting and says that it is because he is done writing, remind him that no one is done until writing time is over and that he needs to think of something else to write or work on his picture a little bit more. Students quickly learn how to add more to their writing while still reaching closure when writing time is officially over for the day.

Brooklyn, age 5 This writing sample is from the first day of independent journal writing. Brooklyn did not realize she could formulate her own sentence, or at least did not want to take a risk and try it, so instead wrote a string of sight words that had been introduced to the class.

Understanding That Writing Should Be Meaningful

Brooklyn's Mini-Lesson: "I see some words on your paper that I know. Can you point to the words and read them to me?" (GLOW) "Hmmm, do those words make sense together?" (GROW) "It looks like you're trying to write something about a bee. What do you want to say?" I made sure Brooklyn could verbalize the idea she wanted to write. Then, I stayed nearby as she got started because I felt she needed the extra support. (SO) Remember, there is no need to have a student erase the first set of words she wrote.

Extending One's Writing

Tip: To improve content and fluency, teach students how to carry on writing about the given topic until writing time is over. By encouraging and expecting them to write more about the topic with which they started, they will indirectly learn how to elaborate and how to include interesting details, not to mention how to stay on topic.

Abby's Mini-Lesson: I asked Abby to read what she had written since I could not read it. "Oh, good idea! You took the words from a different story and made your own sentence. Very creative." (GLOW) "What kind of book is looking at you? Is it one of your favorites?" (GROW) "Tell me more about it!" (SO)

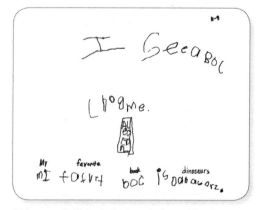

Abby, age 6 This student wrote *I see a book looking at me.* When I encouraged her to write more about it, the result was a second sentence that is much more meaningful and clearly demonstrates the student's ability to hear and separate sounds in words.

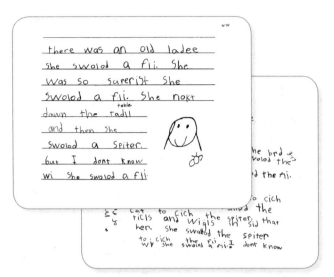

Developing Fluency and Stamina

In addition to being a good way to assess comprehension and the ability to retell a story, assigning a recently shared book as the daily writing topic almost always results in students writing more than they might otherwise because they often try to write out the entire story. This indirectly improves their stamina and their fluency.

Thom, age 5 After seeing the book and hearing the song "There Was an Old Lady Who Swallowed a Fly" this student wrote the singsong series of cumulative events. He continued to write another page, adding his own funny ending: "Maybe she liks the tast of flis."

Sentence Structure

Your modeling of the writing of complete and grammatically correct sentences during the first six weeks of school will help tremendously with students' sentence sense and their ability to write sentences on their own. However, as the months go on and they begin to write longer and more complex sentences, the chances of making grammatical errors will increase. With this age level, it is not appropriate to expect students' sentences to be always grammatically correct. Many of them do not yet speak in complete, fluent sentences, and since writing is just talk written down, their writing will sound like five-year-old speech.

Most grammatical mistakes at this age are developmental, meaning that they will eventually correct themselves over time, so it is not necessary to spend a lot of time explaining to students why the way something is worded is incorrect. Instead, when you see mistakes in sentence structure, read back what the student has written and then restate the sentence with a more standard phrasing. The student may pick up on it and change his or her writing accordingly. If not, leave it be.

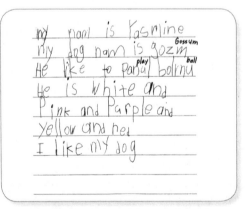

Yasmine, age 5 Yasmine did not use proper subject-verb agreement (*dog name* and *he like*), most likely because she was writing words she knew how to spell and had not yet learned that she could add sounds to the end.

Learning That Writing Should Sound Like Talking

Yasmine's Mini-Lesson: "I can read this all by myself because you used such good sounds." (GLOW) I read the piece out loud exactly as it is. "Did anything sound funny to you?" (GROW) "Remember, writing should sound just like the way we talk. After you write an idea, be sure to go back and read it carefully to see if it says exactly what you wanted it to say." I assist Yasmine with rereading the piece and finding and correcting the two words that need an *s*. (SO)

Trying Novel Words and Sentences

Initially students will write sentences in their journals that are similar to those you've modeled in whole-class lessons during the first six weeks of school. Since your purpose at that time was to use some familiar words along with one or two words with obvious phonemes, it was necessary to control the vocabulary of the sentences. Not only will students' sentences sound contrived at first, such as *I can see a pumpkin*, but it will become apparent that many students are very comfortable writing these known words and are not having to think or risk as much as they should be during writing time. This is not a sign that your students are lazy, uninspired, or cautious about trying something new; what they need now are a few ideas that will indirectly give them permission to write different types of sentences.

Lori, age 5 Lori's writing reflects her limited repertoire of sentence starters.

Typically, students will naturally move from writing sentences with a controlled vocabulary to writing more natural sounding sentences; however, if they do not, it may be necessary to make a temporary rule that sentences in journals can no longer start with *I see . . .*, *I like . . .*, or other commonly used sentence patterns in your classroom. Once students start trying other ways to begin their sentences, they will soon drop the tendency to always write *I see . . .* and *I like. . . .*

Lori's Mini-Lesson: "I like how you wrote some words that we have learned." (GLOW) "What else can you say about the red apple besides that you see it?" (GROW) "Write one more idea and then I'll come back and read it." (SO) Lori added *And I like red apples*, which showed progress because the words *and* and *like* had not yet been introduced and were therefore not known words.

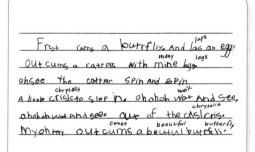

Reading Back One's Writing to Ensure Meaning and Accuracy

Jozette, age 5 This student has written lyrics to a song the students learned in class while studying caterpillars and butterflies. Having students write out a song encourages the practice of going back and reading what was written because students tend to sing and re-sing the song as they write, which involves a lot of rereading.

ESTABLISHING AN IMPORTANT WRITING HABIT

Be sure to constantly model pointing and reading back what is written as a way for students to check that their writing actually says what they intended it to say. Let students know that even adults go back and reread what they have written. As you circulate, if you come upon a student whose writing does not make sense, ask, "Can you read this to me?" This will allow the student to discover on his or her own that what was written doesn't sound right. Also, I will periodically say out loud, to the entire class, "I want everyone to stop, point to your words and read them, and be sure they make sense. Everyone, do that now."

Periods as End Marks

As the year progresses, kindergarten students will become aware that writing contains marks other than letters. They will also notice that sometimes it is appropriate to use capital letters. These conventions of writing are good topics for individualized mini-lessons as long as there are not more pressing instructional needs such as sound segmentation, sound-letter correspondence, spacing between words, sentence formation, and staying on topic.

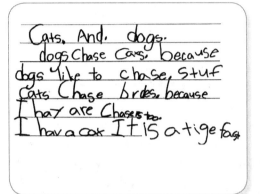

Josefina, age 5 This student tried to use periods in her writing following recent feedback on how to improve her writing. Though there are more pressing issues with her writing, such as more consistent spacing between words and improved handwriting, it was important to notice and comment about how she experimented with periods. Also, once students start putting periods in their writing it opens the door to working on getting end punctuation in the correct places.

Experimenting With Periods

Tip: When students start to use periods, they often put a period after every word or at the end of each line of writing. Reminders that sentences do not always end right at the ends of lines and individualized mini-lessons similar to the ones below will help students get a better understanding of where end punctuation goes.

Josefina's Mini-Lesson: "I see that you put some periods in your writing, just like I asked you to when I talked to you about your writing score. That's great!" (GLOW) "I'm going to read this to you and I'll stop every time I come to one of your periods. You tell me which parts sound right." I read the writing as it is, stopping at all the periods. (GROW) "Now, I'll read it again. This time I'll stop only when it seems like I should stop. And that is where I want you to stick a period in. Ready?" (SO)

Addy's Mini-Lesson: "Wow! Not only did you use periods in your writing, but you got all of them in the right places." (GLOW) "Do you remember that sentences are supposed to start with capital letters?" (GROW) "Let me teach you an easy way to get your capital letters in the right places, too. Just remember that after a period you always have to put a capital letter. You can think of it like a pattern if you want to: period, capital, period, capital. Why don't you see if you can do that right now? You can erase some lowercase letters if you need to." (SO)

Addy, age 5 It is evident that this student knows where to put periods. The next skill to teach her is to capitalize the beginning of sentences.

Chapter Seven

Supplementing Daily Writing Instruction

Thirty minutes of daily journal writing with the built-in support of individualized mini-lessons will result in your kindergarten students making rapid and steady progress in the development of their writing skills. You will likely choose, however, to supplement journal writing time with additional instruction in key concepts and skills necessary for emergent writers and readers. The time you devote to any additional instruction will not only further develop your students' writing skills but their reading skills will improve in a similar fashion and their confidence and enthusiasm for school and learning in general will be off to a great and presumably enduring start.

Because there are so many possibilities for supplementing writing instruction, the intent of this chapter is not to list and discuss every possible activity you might use outside of journal writing time. Nor is the aim to imply what absolutely has to occur instructionally in order for students to be successful writers by the end of their kindergarten year. Rather, included here are just a handful of some of the most successful, tried-and-true ideas I've found for enhancing what already occurs during daily writing. The hope is that you find at least a few new ideas to add to your instructional repertoire.

USING STUDENT NAMES TO TEACH LETTERS, SOUNDS, AND CHUNKS

Students are always interested in their names and learning the letters that make up their names. Almost equally appealing are the names of their classmates. Use this to your advantage by creating classroom activities and games that draw your students' attention to analyzing the spelling of their own and each other's names.

Playing a Daily Name Game to Teach the Names of Letters

One highly effective activity is playing a daily name-spelling game when choosing the special student or helper for the day. Do a preliminary lesson within the first few days of school to introduce and visually display the number of letters in each student's name, such as a graphing activity in which each letter of a student's name falls in a single graph square. Have the name graph handy or be sure the student name cards or a list of student names is visible in your group gathering area. Each day, choose a name from your class list to be the special helper and let students guess who it is. Say something along the lines of, "The special helper for today has *six* letters in his or her name."

Draw six lines on the board or chart paper, one for each letter, and encourage students to try and guess the letters that make up the name. If a student guesses a letter that is in the name you have chosen, write the letter on the appropriate line. If the letter is not in the name, write it in another area. Doing so will ensure that each letter that is guessed results in learning as the students see the letter associated with the guess, watch you form it correctly, and refer to the group of letters for subsequent guesses. All you must do is simply focus on facilitating students' guesses and writing letters on the board, on or away from the lines. The point of the game is to practice thinking about and using letters, not who wins or loses. Students will always win because they will eventually discover the helper's name.

This game will take approximately 10 minutes during the first several weeks of school. Most students will just guess random letters; others will want to join in the game but will not know any letter names. Your job will be to encourage them to raise their hands, sing the alphabet song so they have some ideas, and encourage them to think of letters in their own name that they might try. Within a couple of weeks, begin teaching them some strategies. If the name has six letters, show them how to count letters in others' names and then guess only letters that appear in the names with six letters. It won't be long until most kindergartners will be able to figure out, by finding and looking at the correct name on the name cards or a list of names, which letters are missing on the lines that are still blank. As students learn the names of letters, understand how to use the class list to make more informed guesses, and learn the spellings of their classmates' names, the guessing will only take a few minutes.

> ### NAMES ARE TEACHING TOOLS
>
> When you receive your class list at the beginning of the year, analyze students' first and last names for common blends, letter chunks, and small words that you plan on teaching, such as *th, ing, er, st,* and *and* (as in Andrew). I have discovered over the years that any blend, chunk, or small word that is found within a student's first or last name will be easily learned, retained, and applied to actual writing by most students in the class.

Extending the Daily Name Game to Teach Letter Sounds and Letter Chunks

In addition to teaching letter names, you can use this activity to work on sound segmentation, letter sounds, and chunking of letters. Once it has been determined who the special helper is, that student can stand before the class and help lead a variety of extension activities. One of the first activities is to have the special helper learn to segment the sounds in his or her name. Begin by modeling how to pull apart the sounds that are heard. Do not refer to the name on the board or any other visual clues initially; this is strictly a listening task used to develop phonemic awareness. If the student's name is Shayna, model how to isolate the sounds, holding up a finger as you say each (see phonemic segmentation procedure, pages 24 and 38): /sh/, /ā/, /n/, /u/. The fact that the name has six letters but only four sounds will be intriguing to the students. Invite the class, including the special helper, to separate and count the sounds with you. Then give Shayna the opportunity to try it by herself.

Next, draw the students' attention back to the board, where *Shayna* is written on the lines. Segment the sounds once again, this time circling the letters that go with them. For the first sound, circle *sh* and explain that these letters are working together to make the /sh/ sound. Do the same with *ay* for the /ā/ sound. The *n* and the last *a* will get their own circles. Your board will look something like the example at right.

Updating and Renewing Discussions about Student Names

Students love this game from day one and will not tire of it as long as you constantly update it and renew the related discussions as the school year progresses. For example, in the beginning the sole objective is to just guess letters and see what transpires. As mentioned above, segmenting, counting, and circling the sounds in names provides ongoing instruction in phonemic awareness and phonics. It won't be long before students are telling you the chunks they hear and see in names instead of you telling them. They will also see small words within names. As students' awareness of letter sounds, letter chunks, and spelling patterns become more heightened as the months go on, the essence of your conversations with them will change.

When most of your students are skilled at deducing the letters in classmates' first names, challenge them to precede their guesses with the terms *capital* or *lowercase*. For example, if a student believes the special helper to be Jacob, he might raise his hand and say, "Is there a capital *J*?" Adding this element to the game will draw students' attention to the fact that all names begin with capital letters and rarely have subsequent capital letters. Another variation that kindergarten students can handle is indicating which blank they are guessing. In this scenario, a student asks, "Is the third letter a lowercase *c*?" Tending to the ordinal positions of letters will assist students in learning to spell names and words accurately. Once students have learned some of the common chunks, permit them to guess groups of letters in names rather than just individual letters. For example, a student might inquire, "Does this name have the *-er* chunk at the end?"

Introducing Last Names for Further Discussions

By January, students will be ready to learn to recognize and write their last names and will enjoy the process of slowly analyzing a new set of names day by day. Switching to last names will result in all kinds of new conversations about sounds, chunks, and spelling patterns, helping to solidify these concepts for your students. Be sure to make new name cards with the students' last names.

Teaching Common Letter Chunks

When a common chunk appears in a student's name, take the time to introduce to the class the "friends" associated with that chunk (see pages 145–149). For example, after analyzing Shayna's name, say, "Oh, I have some friends I want you to meet." Show The Good Boys card (page 145), tell the kids the names of the friends on the card (students are always excited to learn these names and try to hear the chunks they contain), and display the card in a place where students can access it. The cards will become a resource for students during writing time. There will be many instances when you will be able to say, "I hear the good boys. Go and look at the good boys and figure out which letters you need."

These and other mnemonic characters that represent blends and tough sound-letter combinations are featured on the reproducible cards on the next few pages. You may recognize *The Icky Twins, The Ow* [also *Ouch*] *Brothers,* and *The Sorry Sisters,* which have been around for many years. (Though they are not my invention, I have been unable to determine and give credit to their original creator.) For our purposes, I have modified a couple slightly: I have changed *The Icky Twins* (*ew* and *ue*) to *The Icky Triplets* (*oo, ew, ue*), because, although the double *o* can make a slightly different sound, it is most often what students need. In addition, I've had great success using *The Bad Boys* (*th*; referred to as such because they make you stick your tongue out), *The Chilly Boys* (*ch*), *The Funny Boys* (*ph*), *The Oi Boys* (*oi, oy*), *The Silent Boys* (*gh*), and *The Whisper Boys* (*wh*). Introduce these slowly as they appear in student names or other words that arise during instruction. By introducing them, keeping the cards handy as resources, and talking about them throughout the year, students will become familiar enough with them to use them in their daily writing and recognize them while decoding during reading.

"FRIENDS" ON YOUR WORD WALL

You can add the cards for The Bad Boys, The Good Boys, and The Whisper Boys to your word wall since there are many high-frequency words that begin with these letter chunks (*the, then, there, they, she, what, when, where, why, who*).

The Bad Boys

Thug  Theo

We make you stick your tongue out.

The Good Boys

Shawn  Shane

We help you be quiet.

The Chilly Boys

Chase  Chuck

We're so ch-ch-chilly!

The Icky Triplets

Drooley   Lew   Sue

The Ow Brothers

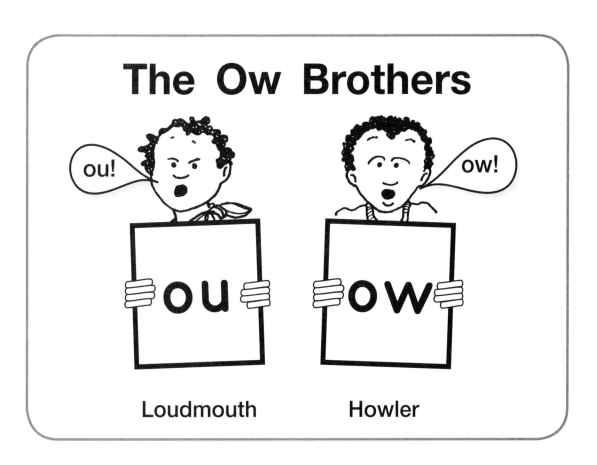

Loudmouth   Howler

The Oi Boys

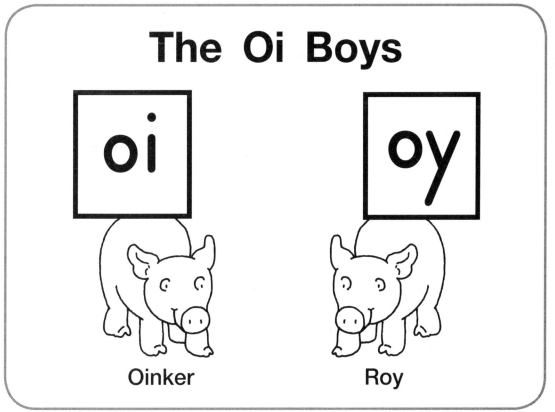

Oinker   Roy

Teaching Writing in Kindergarten © 2008 by Randee Bergen, Scholastic Teaching Resources

The Silent Boys

Hugh  Dwight

We don't say much.

The Whisper Boys

Whit  White

The Funny Boys

Phil 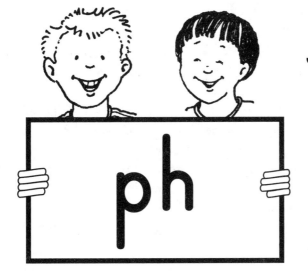 Joseph

ph makes the *f* sound—how funny!

The Sorry Sisters

Audrey   Dawn

SUPPORTING WRITING INSTRUCTION THROUGH SHARED READING EXPERIENCES

The time you devote to teaching reading will positively affect students' writing development, just as instruction and practice in writing clearly has a positive impact on reading development. It makes sense, then, to intentionally bring writing instruction into the time allotted for shared reading (teacher-led reading from a purposely chosen big book or chart while the students follow along). During this activity, you may introduce print conventions, teach vocabulary, encourage predictions, and develop decoding and comprehension skills.

Teachers sometimes read the same big book repeatedly, addressing different teaching points with each subsequent reading. Using the same book for several different lessons makes it easy to devote at least one day's reading to the development of writing skills. Most big books that work well for shared reading do so because they have large print, picture clues that match the text, and a combination of 1) high-frequency words and 2) words that require the use of beginning decoding skills (the same two categories of words you will encourage your students to use during writing time). Because of this, it is easy to address reading objectives and writing objectives with the same shared reading material.

Emphasizing Concepts of Print

One way to incorporate writing instruction into shared reading time is to point out to students some of the things the author did in the book and to help them realize that they, too, can try these techniques since they are writers and authors. For example, you may want to emphasize directionality, and remind students that writers, even authors of big books, always go in the right direction. If they didn't, it sure would be hard to read their books! Other connections between books and students' own writing include but are not limited to: spacing between words, using known words, making sure pictures and words complement each other, punctuation, capitalization, legible writing, speech bubbles, staying on topic, the meaning of extra-large and bold print, genres, choice of titles, and unique and interesting ideas. The possibilities are almost endless.

Introducing Word Wall Words

Perhaps the most useful way to use shared reading to enhance writing development is to choose books or charts that will help you introduce the high-frequency words or important letter chunks that kindergartners should learn to recognize (for example, *-ing, -all, -er*). As discussed in Chapter 2, frequently used sight words should be formally introduced to the class and added to the word wall. Doing so makes it possible for you to expect that certain words be spelled correctly. The word wall provides a resource for students, allowing them to successfully follow through with your expectation.

Although by no means an all-inclusive list, the titles included on page 152 are excellent ones to use to introduce and/or review the common high-frequency sight words typically introduced to young readers and writers. Notice that not all of the titles are big books; some are nursery rhymes or commonly known songs or poems. Associating each sight word with one or more specific titles will help students recall that a particular word has been introduced to the class and that therefore they know that word. Recollection of the title, and the discussion that accompanied it, will also assist students in committing the spelling of the word to memory. Drawing students' attention to the particular sight word or chunk of letters that is going to be introduced via the shared reading should usually occur during subsequent readings of the book rather than during the first reading, although this is not always possible due to time restraints.

Once you've read a big book and students are familiar with the story, pictures, and whatever reading skill(s) you introduced with the text, draw their attention to the high-frequency word you want to introduce. The word should appear several times in the book so the students have the opportunity to search for it and read it automatically as they come upon it. Talk about what it is about the word that makes it possible for the students to recognize it. If, for example, the chosen word is *they*, help students to see that the word starts with *the* and then has a *y* at the end. Or, if the *-ay* chunk has been introduced, discuss how *they* sounds like it should have the *-ay* chunk but does not. These discussions will help students memorize how to spell the word and then transfer that knowledge to their journal writing.

TEACHING HANDWRITING

Correct letter formation is key to students' writing being legible and to students being proud of their work. It is also important that handwriting develop in sync with the other beginning skills of writing. Any teacher who has taught a grade beyond kindergarten knows that it is next to impossible to change a student's letter formation once it has become routine.

Supervised Small-Group Practice

The best way to support the development of permanent proper letter formation is to provide direct instruction and allow only supervised practice in handwriting. During the first half of the school year, kindergarten students benefit from small-group instruction for handwriting. Gather seven or eight students at most around you or with an appropriately trained instructional aide. Provide paper or individual dry erase boards for each student. Have in mind specific letters or, even better, two or three sight words to practice. Review letter formation by having students repeat the handwriting cues for the letter that is about to be written (see pages 43–45). The students can say the cue with you as they write the letter in the air with gross motor movements. Then, have students write the letter on the papers or dry erase boards that are before them.

Observe each student carefully, calling attention to errors in formation either before they happen (for example, when it is obvious a student is going to start a letter at the bottom instead of the top), as they happen (a student lifts his pencil to make the curve on the *r* instead of tracing back up the stick), or immediately after they happen. Learn to look for the telltale signs that a letter was wrongly formed. For instance, an *o* that was started at the bottom rather than the top will usually not be perfectly round and hooked together, and it might have a crossing of beginning and ending points at the bottom. An *m* that had the stick added as an afterthought will have a disconnected flick of a pencil mark somewhere near the left or top of the letter. Do not accept any incorrectly formed letters from students during handwriting practice. And emphasize that you expect them to make these letters in just the same manner when they are writing on their own. Remind them that you will be looking for this as you walk around during journal writing time.

Shared Reading Titles
Used to Introduce High-Frequency Words

Title	Author and/or Publisher	Word(s), Letter Chunks
Shopping	Wright Group/Sunshine	*a*
Hey Diddle, Diddle	nursery rhyme	*the*
All I Am	Eileen Roe	*I, am*
I Went Walking	Sue Williams and Julie Vivas	*I, see, me*
Brown Bear, Brown Bear	Bill Martin and Eric Carle	*I, see, me*
School Bus	Donald Crews	*stop*
The Gingerbread Man	many different versions	*can*
I Can Read	Creative Teaching Press	*can*
One Potato, Two Potato	handclapping rhyme	*one*
There Were Ten in the Bed	Mary Gruetzke	*in, there*
Little Bo Peep	nursery rhyme	*little*
Little Boy Blue	nursery rhyme	*little*
Little Miss Muffet	nursery rhyme	*little*
The Little Red Hen	Byron Barton	*little, not, will*
10 Apples Up on Top	Dr. Seuss	*up, on*
Old King Cole	nursery rhyme	*he, was, -ing*
There Was an Old Woman	nursery rhyme	*she, was*
Cat and Dog	Creative Teaching Press	*and*
The Wheels on the Bus	song	*and*
What's the Weather Like Today?	Rozanne Lanczak Creative Teaching Press	*like*
Where's Your Tooth?	Creative Teaching Press	*your*
Happy Birthday	song	*to, you*
Twinkle, Twinkle Little Star	nursery rhyme	*are, -ar*
Roses Are Red	nursery rhyme	*are*
Pledge of Allegiance		*of*
Who Will Help?	Creative Teaching Press	*will, not*
Jack and Jill	nursery rhyme	*-ill*
Peter, Peter, Pumpkin Eater	nursery rhyme	*-er*
Cat and Dog	Creative Teaching Press	*too, -oo*
I Love You	rebus poem	*love*
Humpty Dumpty	nursery rhyme	*all, -all*
Once I Caught a Fish Alive	finger play	*once*
Just This Once	Wright Group/Sunshine	*once*
Eency, Weency Spider	nursery rhyme	*-ou, -ow*
Because of a Sneeze	MacMillan/Bernice Myers	*because, of*

Integrating Phonemic Awareness, Phonics, and Spelling Into Handwriting Practice

The time spent on handwriting practice is most beneficial when the reading and writing of sight words is incorporated into the instruction. Kindergarten students do not usually have formal spelling lists to learn, but they do need to learn to spell common sight words. They can practice spelling while receiving instruction in letter formation. For example, if students practice writing the word *and* with your instruction and supervision, you can integrate sound segmentation (phonemic awareness), letter names and letter-sound correspondence (phonics), letter formation, and the reading and correct spelling of the word. A sample lesson is shown below.

Sample Small-Group Handwriting Lesson

Sound Segmentation

"Today we're going to practice writing the word *and*. Let's start by listening to and counting the sounds in the word *and*. Watch me. My turn: *aaa* (I put up my index finger), *nnn* (next my middle finger), *d*" (then my ring finger).

"How many sounds did you hear in *and*? You're right—three. Okay. Let's try it all together. Your turn. Start with zero. Zero is a fist."

I repeat the elongation of each sound, listening to students and being sure they correctly raise one finger for each sound.

"Does anyone want to try it all by him- or herself?"

Phonics

"Now let's listen to just the first sound: *aaa*. What letter will we write for *aaa*? Yes, we'll write the letter *a*."

Letter Formation

"Does anyone remember how letter *a* goes? What do we say when we write letter *a* to make sure it turns out looking right? That's close. We say, 'make a *c*, go up, down.' Let's use our magic finger and write an *a* in the air. Say it with me: 'make a *c*, go up, down.' Great! One more time, just to be sure we know how to do it. I'll be watching you."

"I think we're ready to write an *a* on our papers. Remember, the letter *a* starts with a *c*. Don't forget to say the words when you write your *a*. That will help your *a* turn out right."

I observe each student making an *a*. I may ask students to make another *a* if I was unable to watch them closely or if they had trouble and need a little extra practice. If students are using dry erase boards, erasing is easy. If they're using paper, erasing is usually not necessary; they can try again in a new spot.

A similar dialogue is repeated for the letters *n* and *d*.

Reading and Spelling

"Okay, let's touch this word and read it. Ready? *and.*"

"Now, let's point to each letter and spell the word. Ready? Touch the *a. . . . a-n-d.*"

Unlined paper rather than lined paper is appropriate for this activity during the first half of the school year. Students should be encouraged to make letters short, tall, or hang down accordingly and this is done just as easily, and sometimes more easily, when there are no lines on the paper.

Supervised Whole-Group Practice

During the second half of the school year, you can move from small-group handwriting practice to whole-group handwriting practice. This handwriting instruction must, however, still be supervised and must be supervised in a manner that allows you to watch all students and provide immediate feedback with the expectation that all letters will be formed correctly. How will you go about this? The best way is to gather students closely on the floor around you and provide individual dry erase boards for each of them. Having students on the floor near you will allow you the opportunity to observe most students' handwriting attempts at once. The dry erase boards are effective because students' writing will be bold and larger than it would be on paper, making it easier for you to see their writing. Also, students can erase quickly and with little effort, meaning that you can make multiple requests of them to erase and try again. A sample whole-group handwriting lesson appears below.

Sample Whole-Group Handwriting Lesson

"Let's talk about the dry erase board rules while we hand out the supplies. Who can remind us of one of the rules?" I lead a brief discussion about the rules (see page 156) while a few helper students pass out the boards, tissues for erasing, and dry erase markers."

"Okay. You just heard the rules. Try your hardest to remember them and follow them so you can keep your supplies the whole time. Should we have our caps off yet? No. We don't even know what we're writing, so it isn't writing time yet."

"Today we're going to write some words with the *-ing* chunk. Who remembers how the *-ing* chunk goes? That's right: *i, n, g.*"

Spelling

"I think we all remember how to make lowercase *i*. It's easy. Go ahead and make a lowercase *i* on your board. Let's talk about *n* and *g* quickly before we write them. We want them to turn out perfectly. First, *n*. Does anyone remember what we say to make *n* turn out perfectly? You're right, 'go down, trace it up, bump.' Everyone, write *n*. I want to hear the words coming out of your mouth while you make the letter."

Letter Formation

"Uh-oh, I see someone who's about to start the letter at the bottom. Do we ever start letters at the bottom? No. Ben, move your marker up by the top of your *i* and start *n* there. Remember, you'll go down first. Oops, Aspen, you didn't trace it up. You lifted your pen and hopped to the top. We don't lift our pens for *n*. Erase your *n* and try it again. This time make sure you really are tracing when you hear your mouth say 'trace it up.'"

I watch each student make an *n* or closely examine the *n*'s of those I was unable to watch to determine if they were written correctly. From my position in a chair, it is fairly easy to observe each student sitting on the floor before me. One student has severe fine motor needs and is unable to write the letters legibly on his own. The student seated next to him knows it is all right to assist him and puts his hand over the other student's hand and to help him move his marker while they say the words together.

"Now we're ready for *g*. We're going to make a *g* in the air, and we have to start with a *c*. Oh no, I see Jake writing on his pants. Is that okay? What will have to happen? Yep, he has to give his supplies to me until he's ready to use them in the right way." Jake pleads to keep his supplies, but then quickly hands them over, knowing the consequence and knowing that he will get another chance.

"Here we go with our *g* in the air: 'make a *c*, go up, trace it down with a hook.' Jake, are you ready to use your supplies correctly? I hope so. Here you go. Okay, class. I want you to say the words, think about them, and make a perfect *g* on your boards."

I stand up so I can carefully observe as many students as possible. "Oops! Is it okay to start *g* at the bottom and go up and around? No. *g* starts with the letter *c*. If you started at the bottom, erase and try again. Say the words. If you need help, I'll say them with you." I ensure that every student has made a correct *g* on his or her board.

Phonemic Awareness and Spelling

"Okay, we've got *ing*! Everyone's *ing* is beautiful. Now, we need to put something in front of the *ing*. Can anyone think of a letter that we can put at the beginning of *ing* to make a real word with the *ing* chunk?" I call on several students and choose one of the suggested letters that the class as a whole needs to work on—*k*.

Letter Formation, Phonemic Awareness, Phonics, and Spelling

The class draws the letter in the air first, saying the letter-formation cue as they go. I watch carefully as the students write the letter *k* on their boards, asking those who form it incorrectly to erase and try it again. Some students check their neighbors' papers to see where to put the *k*.

As students get the entire word written neatly on their boards, I call out their names or say "erase," signaling to them that they are finished, have formed all the letters correctly, and are ready to erase and get ready for the next word. When all boards are clear, I know I have provided sufficient instruction and feedback and all students have gained closure at this point. The lesson continues with two more -*ing* words, but the students are expected to write the -*ing* chunk without going through the steps of writing the letters in the air together before writing it on their boards. Integrating the spelling of a rime and the concept of word families addresses phonemic awareness, phonics, and spelling during handwriting practice.

Lesson Materials

You will need dry erase boards, tissues or old socks for erasing, and dry erase markers. Small dry erase boards (as small as 4 ½-by-6 inches) are available at teacher supply stores or through teacher supply catalogs. The nonmagnetic ones are fairly reasonable in price and hold up well for several years. The magnetic boards are more expensive but can also be used for phonics and spelling activities that involve magnetic letters. If you do not have enough boards for each student in your class, students can share boards. You will have to teach them how to cooperate by taking turns writing every other letter. If your school does not have dry erase markers in the supply room, you'll want to add these as a standard item on the student school supply list. Also, I have each student contribute two boxes of tissue because we use more tissues with this activity than we do for wiping noses.

Before beginning whole-group handwriting practice with dry erase boards, it will be necessary to establish some ground rules on the use of dry erase boards. Enforcing the rules will afford you more actual teaching time and lessen the time you spend managing twenty-plus students in close quarters with markers. See the box below for expectations for using dry erase boards and markers. These rules do not need to be posted. They just need to be reiterated, in simple language that students can understand, each and every time you pass out the supplies. If this is to be productive teaching time, students must adhere to these expectations. It is easy to get students to do so—just take their supplies away immediately when they do not follow the rules. If you must take a student's supplies—and you will need to do so for the first several times you gather students for this activity, but rarely thereafter—ask the student after a few moments if he or she is ready to follow the rules and use the dry erase board the right way. Then give the supplies back to the student so he or she can continue to participate and practice handwriting.

RULES FOR USING DRY ERASE BOARDS AND MARKERS

1. Take the cap off your dry erase marker only when the teacher says it is time to write. Store the cap on the top end of your marker so it does not get lost.

2. Do not sniff the markers.

3. Do not write until the teacher tells you to write. Only write what you are supposed to write. Do not draw pictures or make designs in between writing what you are supposed to write.

4. Do not write on your skin, your clothes, your erasing tissue or sock, the carpet, the edge of the dry erase board, or your neighbor. Write only on the dry erase board.

5. Write big enough that the teacher can see your work, but not so big that the whole board gets messy.

6. Erase what you have written as soon as the teacher tells you to erase. That is your signal that you did a good job and wrote the letter/word the way in which you were supposed to. A clean board is a signal to the teacher that you are ready to write the next thing.

7. Try to write the letter/word on your own, but if you need to look around the room for clues or watch your neighbor write it, that's okay.

SUPPORTING STRUGGLING STUDENTS

At any point in the school year you may find that a particular student is stuck in one place in his or her writing development and is not, despite your daily individualized mini-lessons, progressing much at all. In these instances, it may be necessary and beneficial to carve out some time for the student to get some one-on-one instruction outside of daily journal writing time. Some examples of students who have required some one-on-one instruction are 1) a student who was not learning the names of the four letters in his name, despite daily instruction and quizzing on the letters during the intense practice of name writing the first six weeks of school; 2) a student who did not learn many letter names or sounds during the first few months of school; and, 3) a student who, despite knowing most of the letter names and sounds, continued day after day to write a string of random letters on her paper.

To move these students along, I establish a short daily time for one-on-one instruction. As with individualized mini-lessons, I keep the instruction brief, about five to ten minutes per session. If you are teaching full-day kindergarten, the down time or rest time that usually occurs after lunch is the perfect time to squeeze in some one-on-one work with students. The room is quiet and peaceful while students rest and look at books, and this provides you the perfect opportunity to give one or two students your (almost) undivided attention. For half-day kindergarten, I usually have the classroom aide conduct these one-on-one interventions, so that I can continue to teach the group during the limited time I have.

Utilizing a Back-and-Forth Notebook

For the first student above, the one who could not remember the names of the four letters in his name, I asked for his parents' support. The child's mother agreed to work with her son at home each evening. The parent and I decided to start a "back and forth notebook," in which both of us would write what activities we did with the student and how effective each activity seemed to be. I worked with the student for about five minutes each day, trying different strategies and activities, and then spent another few minutes writing about the activities, noting which ones seemed to work particularly well. In the notebook, I modeled what type of information the child's mother should include when she wrote to me as well as how to scaffold the instruction and expectations so it got a little more challenging each day. She caught on quickly. Within a week, the student could name the four letters in his name on a consistent basis, even when the letters were presented out of order. We were so thrilled with the success that we continued the "back-and-forth notebook" for most of the school year. This provided extra support and instruction for the student in all subject areas and helped him become a proficient kindergarten writer by the end of the year.

A back-and-forth notebook entry shows my correspondence with the mother of a student who needed extra literacy support at home.

Teaching Letters and Sounds With Alphabet Flashcards

There is a highly effective, tried-and-true method for getting most students to more quickly learn the names and sounds of letters. Either make or purchase a set of alphabet flashcards. The purchased ones will more than likely include a picture for each letter, which will be helpful for this intervention. Be sure, however, that all pictures represent the true sound of each letter and that, hopefully, the pictures represent the short sounds of the vowels. You will need to find five-to-ten minutes each day for an instructional aide, a parent, a volunteer, or yourself to work with the student one-on-one.

Start with the letter *Aa* and model how to trace the capital letter while saying the letter name, trace the lowercase letter while saying the letter's sound, and then touch the picture and say its name, emphasizing and elongating the beginning sound of the picture. The student will do this daily, with just a few letters at the beginning of the intervention and then more letters during each session as the student becomes faster at it. Initially, the student should progress through the letters in alphabetical order; but, as he or she begins to memorize them in a particular order, the letters should be presented randomly. After the third or fourth session, when the student knows the routine, begin to expect the student to trace the letters using proper letter formation. That is, be sure he or she starts tracing at the top of most letters and goes down rather than up. It works well to put the alphabet flashcards on a ring and to let the student keep the ring of cards nearby during daily writing time so he or she can refer to them and more easily apply what he or she has been learning during the one-on-one time.

Using the Two-Word Combination Strategy

Sometimes students do not catch on to sound segmentation and sound-letter correspondence very quickly and may need some concentrated one-on-one assistance to move from random letter spelling with no spacing to partially phonetic spelling with spaces between words. This brief one-on-one writing activity, to be done at a time other than daily writing time, is effective for this situation. Provide scratch paper for the student and have him or her write two-word phrases or labels, where the first word is a word the student knows (because it is a word that has officially been introduced to the class and placed on the word wall) and the second word is a word that will require listening to the sounds. Examples include *the horse*, *a man*, and *my cat*. Notice that the second word in these phrases (the one that will require the student to listen to the sounds) always has phonemes that are easy to distinguish and write the corresponding letters for. When you give the student a two-word combination to write, remind him or her that the first word is a known word and that he or she can either just write it or can find and copy it from the word wall. If the student does not yet know how to write *a* and *the*, he or she should know them quite well after a few weeks of this.

Next, ask the student if the second word is on the word wall or if it is a word for which he or she will need to listen to the sounds. Help the student segment the sounds; both of you should have your hands up and use your fingers to determine how many sounds there are. Determine if the student can isolate the first sound and if he or she knows which letter to write. If the student knows neither, help with this so he or she is sure of exactly what needs to be written. Before writing, remind the student that since the first word is finished—*a* or *the*—the student will need to put a finger space. Be sure the student leaves his or her finger on the paper in the correct place until the pencil is actually in place on the paper to begin the next word. Watch the student write the first letter of the second word. If the student indicates that he or she has written the word and does not sense a need to put down any more sounds, stop here. Have the student point to the words and read back what was written. If the student wrote *the m* for *the man* then he or she should read it as *the man*. Since the point of this task is to move into partially phonetic spelling it is not necessary to put down all or even more than one of the sounds for the second word. Just getting the student to space between words and write a letter that makes sense for the word he or she is attempting to write is the goal. Be sure to expect the student to transfer this skill to daily journal writing time. When the student can do it with just a little assistance from you, the next step is for the student to apply it while writing independently.

References

Arends, M. Conversation with Randee Bergen. (2004).

Bruner, J. S., & Sherwood, V. (1975). Peekaboo and the learning of rule structures.
In J. S. Bruner & K. Sylva (Eds.), *Play: Its role in development and evolution* (pp. 277–285).
Harmondsworth, England: Penguin Books.

Feldgus, E. G., & Cardonick, I. (1999). *Kid writing: A systematic approach to phonics, journals, and writing workshop.* Bothell, WA: The Wright Group.

Galperin, P. Y. (1992). Organization of mental activity and the effectiveness of learning.
Journal of Russian and East European Psychology, 30(4), 65–82.

Gentry, J. R. (2000). *The literacy map.* New York: Mondo.

Gentry, J. R. (2004). *The science of spelling: The explicit specifics that make great readers and writers (and spellers!).* Portsmouth, NH: Heinemann.

Stauffer, R. (1980). *The language experience approach to the teaching of reading.* New York: Harper & Row.

Vygotsky, L. S. (1978). *Mind in society: The development of higher psychological processes.* Cambridge, MA: Harvard University Press.